D1631371

FAVOURITES

FAVOURITES

A personal selection
by

DAME SYBIL THORNDIKE

HODDER AND STOUGHTON
LONDON SYDNEY AUCKLAND TORONTO

Dame Sybil Thorndike and the publishers wish to thank the following for permission to use copyright material in this book:

The Society of Authors as the literary representative of the Estate of John Masefield for 'Twilight' and an extract from 'The Everlasting Mercy'.

The Society of Authors, on behalf of the Bernard Shaw Estate, for 2 extracts from 'Saint Joan'.

The Clarendon Press Oxford, for 2 poems by Robert Bridges: 'Nightingales' and 'A Passer-By'.

J. M. Dent & Sons Ltd and the Trustees for the copyrights of the late Dylan Thomas, for 'The Rev. Eli Jenkins' Prayer' from 'Under Milk Wood'.

Macmillan Publishing Co. Inc., New York, for 9 verses from 'I heard Christ Sing' from the Collected Poems of Hugh MacDiarmid.

M. B. Yeats and the Macmillan Company of Basingstoke and London for 3 poems by W. B. Yeats: 'When You Are Old', 'The Lake Isle of Innisfree' and 'Down by the Salley Gardens'.

Macmillan Company of Basingstoke and London for 2 poems by James Stephens: 'Little Things' and 'The Rivals'.

George Allen & Unwin Ltd for 3 extracts from Euripides, translated by Gilbert Murray: from 'The Hippolytus', 'Medea' and 'The Trojan Women'.

CONTENTS

FOREWORD

In my selection of some of my favourite poems — those that are my *real* favourites in all the world — it has been necessary for me to choose only a few, because I love so many! I have chosen largely those that meant most to me and Lewis.

I have never really thought in terms of 'favourites' when it comes to poetry. I just know the poems I like, and do them. So deeply rooted is this love for verse that I can hardly analyse it — it is an intuitive thing.

From a child I have always enjoyed jingly verse — nursery rhymes or any verse that had rhythm in it. That is probably why I cannot swallow much modern verse today, its rhythm is more like that of prose. I admire it but I prefer the older verse with traditional rhyme and rhythm.

At school I came to love Shakespeare — the plays only — we did not do the sonnets, and in fact I don't remember doing much poetry at all. My father used to read Shakespeare to us from quite an early age. I can always hear him reading *Hamlet* and he looked so like Forbes Robertson that my brother and I were thrilled. He had that quality of face — the ascetic type.

When I left school at thirteen to concentrate on my piano studies I had to have private tuition. In particular my piano music with its wonderful rhythms and melodies gave me the ability to appreciate the music of words. But it was not until a good deal later, when I was twenty-one, that poetry became a passion. Meanwhile I learnt to appreciate a great deal of prose. As a girl of fourteen and fifteen I adored Thomas Carlyle, especially his *French Revolution* and *On Heroes, Hero-Worship and the Heroic.* When I was fifteen the mother of one of my piano pupils made me very keen on reading. But in reality it was the piano all the time, with little room for anything else in my teens.

Music is also a thing that is intuitive. You accept it unconsciously and dwell in the realm of the emotions. So I spent all my teens with piano music, training, practising, performing, teaching; but not developing as a whole person. As a result I was a very late developer — still a child at sixteen even though I was then teaching music pupils. But I had led a sheltered life at home with my parents which perhaps explains this.

My parents were both wonderful natural musicians. Father was an Anglican priest — and I grew up with hymns and psalms— and learnt to love many. Again it was the rhythms that held me. And there was the Bible with its drama and beauty. Isaiah, with his great declamatory phrases — in the Authorised Version of course. I can't stand the others — was a favourite. Here I found the wonderful sounds and rhythms of free verse. Then the Psalms; I knew them all and read one daily. I can still hear my father singing them from the Psalter on Sundays, kneeling in the aisle, intoning one verse with the congregation responding with the next. There are so many I like: Psalm 23 'The Lord is my shepherd: therefore can I lack nothing', Psalm 51 'Have mercy upon me, O God, after thy great goodness', and especially Psalm 137 'By the waters of Babylon we sat down and wept: when we remembered thee, O Sion. As for our harps, we hanged them up: upon the trees that are therein. For they that led us away captive required of us then a song, and melody in our heaviness: "Sing us one of the songs of Sion." How shall we sing the Lord's song: in a strange land?' I think that Psalms in the *Book of Common Prayer* are the most beautiful poems. The men who translated these Psalms were poets themselves.

But poetry really entered my life when I started my stage career in California with the Ben Greet Company, which played Shakespeare, old comedy and the old shepherd plays. I was twenty-one, and had never been away from home or alone before, so I was terribly homesick. One of the actors in the company, Eric Blind, was mad keen on poetry, especially Browning. He used to say that "all other poets are like thin gravy compared to his thick soup"! Through him I suddenly discovered a new world, and this helped me to overcome a good deal of my unhappiness. All the passion that I had previously put into my piano playing, was now channelled into two things: acting and poetry. I found that whatever time I had free from studying my part or learning Shakespeare, I wanted to spend reading verse.

Indeed America proved to be an eye-opener to me. I had found a new career after the collapse of my ambitions as a pianist due to over-straining my wrist. I had no family around me and I was at last finding things out for myself. Poetry came as something precious, particularly in my leisure hours. So with Browning, Shelley and Keats to start me on my journey, I had their collected poems as my 'bible'. One of the first poems that gripped me was 'To a Skylark' by Shelley, after which came 'Ode to the West Wind', then 'Ode to a Nightingale' by Keats. I discovered, from reading the lives of the poets, that all three lived at the same time. Studying the lives of the poets has helped me to understand and present their poems better.

Rhythm had always been important to me, from my earliest years, but it was now rhyme that held me, with the English poets. This is probably why I am not so keen on free verse, though I find blank verse very satisfying because of its wonderful beat. I particulary liked the Alexandrian verse that Gilbert Murray used in his translations of the Greeks. You will see I have slipped in some from Euripides for that reason, and another of my favourite plays: *St Joan* by George Bernard Shaw.

It was in my early twenties that I first met Lewis Casson the man that I married. He had a deep love for poetry also. When I first knew him in Manchester we used to go for long walks together in the Derbyshire hills, or around Northenden and the outskirts of Manchester that are all built up now. We would walk and talk and learn poetry. He helped me with the phrasing of lines more than anyone in my whole life.

Lewis could not bear what he called the English 'droop', the dropping of the voice at the end of a phrase so that the last word is lost. He would mark poems carefully in pencil, indicating intonation and phrasing, pauses and pitch. Our verses were covered in hieroglyphics, and he maintained that one should never come down to the keynote until the very last line. The voice could come to a half-close but never to the keynote. I used to practise this by reading the morning paper to him at breakfast. I had to read the leading article, making quite sure that my voice never dropped until the end. I had to learn to keep the tension up, as in music, until the final chord.

I had never analysed sounds like this before. It was a revelation and appealed to me as a musician tremendously. Eric Blind in America had read poetry to me, but never like this. Lewis had a musician's ear, and the Welsh lilt and sense of vigour and oratory made the poems so beautiful. He unfolded not only poetry but plays also. I had done Shakespeare before I met him, but working with him on the plays was an inspiration.

Eventually Lewis and I began to give public poetry readings. I remember the first occasion was at a hall in Deansgate, Manchester. We used to read verse in the Working Men's Clubs at Ancoats, which was the slum area, and we did plays as well. This started before I became engaged to Lewis, probably when I was twenty-four or five. Soon, wherever we were booked to do a play, we usually had a booking for a recital, so when we were on tour we would do both. Since then we have been round the world twice, including poetry in our repertoire. It has indeed been a part of our life together. These are my favourites as well as his.

THE POEMS

I would like to say a few words about the poems I have chosen. They are simple, because I am a woman who prefers simple things. In other words this is not a scholar's choice but a lover's. Every word and pause in these verses is a familiar old friend. I have kept the selection in a basic chronological order, moving from the Greeks to the more modern verse.

When I was introduced to the plays of Euripides as translated by Gilbert Murray, I was absolutely knocked sideways by them. This setting of the Greek tragedies was something entirely new to me. The play in question was the *Hippolytus* and we were presenting it in Manchester. I was only the goddess, a part which I thought would be very easy until I discovered it wasn't! But what especially caught my attention was the chorus: "Could I take me to some cavern for mine hiding..." Probably my most famous Euripidean roles were Hecuba in *The Trojan Women* and the title role in *Medea*.

Many of the older poems I love are anonymous. The first one in this section, 'Lestenyt, lordynges, both elde and yinge' was the one that I spoke as the Angel Gabriel in *The Star of Bethlehem*, a play built on the old Shepherd plays, by Professor Gayley. This was my very first acting job, performed in California with the Ben Greet Company. 'In somer when the shawes be sheyne' is a favourite because of its lovely rhythms — and what the poem means, verse four especially. 'I sing of a Maiden' is very well known but has unusual rhythm and beautiful sense. 'Balow, my babe' is one of those poems that I have used a great deal. It is such a piece of character writing: with the last verse putting men in their rightful place!

'The Old Cloak' Lewis and I would do together as a conversation between man and wife in a peasant dialect. Lewis's Welsh accent would become very strong. The old man in the poem is so stubborn — until the very end.

You will see I have chosen a number of old Scottish ballads. My Grandfather was a northern Scot from Aberdeen, and many of these he knew and loved. 'The Bonnie House of Airlie' shows the spirit of the old clan feuds; and I think 'The Seven Virgins' is delightful, with its plea for charity tacked on the end:

> Amen, good Lord; and your charity
> Is the ending of my song.

For humour again, 'Two Rivers' is neat and beautifully expressed. There are many versions of 'Barbara Allen' but this is my favourite, taken from the *Oxford Book of English Verse*. 'Waly, Waly' is so sad — I do this with a Scottish dialect, a sense of keening in my voice, and 'The Queen's Marie' also. I have known this poem since my childhood. It was one of my grandfather's favourites which he used to read to me. Very unsuitable for a young girl! I would cry and cry over it, particularly the last verses which he would sing. I can recall still the haunting melody.

'Praise of Women' is one of the oldest poems I have included, but it is still at the top of my list. I use it frequently when I am asked to say some poetry in public. Here is not only lovely sound and rhythm but absurdity also. 'Lament for the Makers' by William Dunbar, is another poem from Scotland that makes me laugh, because it is ridiculous. The woman is such an old misery — though a 'believer'.

What can I say about 'Give me my scallop shell of quiet'? It is a very precious poem by Sir Walter Raleigh. He wrote it the night before he was executed when he was imprisoned in the Gateway going into Dean's Yard, Westminster.

Edmund Spenser's 'In Praise of Eliza' is quite charming. I think we have here a teacher talking to the girls about (Queen) Eliza and telling them to behave as well as she does. The last verse is especially prim — organising everyone with the promise of treats and the 'goodbye now, you are dismissed' sort of thing.

Naturally I have included a lot of Shakespeare's poetry; the songs from his plays and some of his sonnets. The songs are among the most beautiful in the world — simple and funny. I never cease to be amazed that a man who could write such violent plays and plumb the vilest human depths, could also write so delicately. The sonnets are superb love songs and, even more, they are love prayers.

Of the Ben Jonson poems 'Epitaph on Salathiel Pavy' is full of pathos. Salathiel was a little thirteen year old chorister at the St James' Chapel Royal and this poem describes the heavenly battle over him. The angels (the Parcae) discovered that he acted

16

and sang so sweetly that heaven got jealous and wanted to keep him!

Robert Herrick's poems on flowers are wonderful and full of vivid description. He makes flowers into people. Look at the last verse of 'To Violets', for instance. Fancy calling them 'poor girls'! Yet his people are also human and 'Delight in Disorder' and 'The Mad Maid's Song' reveal a depth of emotion.

From John Milton I have chosen, among other things, part of 'Samson Agonistes I', for this is Milton at his most violent and best. I'm sorry to say I don't like Milton (because he was horrid to Mrs Milton) but he could write! And my father loved his work and recited it to us when we were young. Even then I thought it was awful. I disliked the cruelty and fierceness. Yet I still feel I must include him among my favourites because there is loveliness amid the sound and fury — particularly in the 'Hymn on the Morning of Christ's Nativity'.

When I think about Shelley and Keats I hardly know where to begin. I find it incredible that I discovered them so late in life. All school children study their poetry as a matter of course today, yet I knew nothing of their poems until I was in my twenties. I am probably not alone though, in finding in their verse an appetiser for poetry in general. After reading them I wanted to press on to other poets. 'Ode to the West Wind' is truly an 'inspiring' poem. I call it a hymn to the Holy Ghost. For this reason I often say it aloud to myself before I am going to do any new work. I love 'To a Skylark' because it has great memories for me of America when I read it for the first time.

So what can I say of Browning whose poetry was perhaps my very first favourite? In a way he tops Shelley and Keats with his humour and depth. I came across a claim in the writings of Robert Louis Stevenson that Browning's *The Ring and the Book* was the 'noblest book of the nineteenth century'. I immediately decided to read it, but discovered it was no easy task because it is an immense tragedy written in blank verse, running into several books. For this reason it is little known, and probably only poets read it. But I persevered with one of the books, *Pompilia*, and was thrilled with it, and learnt it by heart. Quite an exercise — but rewarding! By contrast my first choice 'Up at a Villa' is Browning at his most lighthearted. I have done it in public many times and its delightful humour and description is always appreciated. I find 'Toccata of Galuppi' full of meaning — and fun. The poet is sighing for the past glories of Venice — the beautiful courtesans of long ago and wondering what sort of life they led. Then 'Memorabilia' sums up just how I felt when I first discovered Shelley and Keats.

Tennyson's rhythm is his great appeal for me — and he comes from the same county as I do — Lincolnshire! My favourite amongst so much of his verse is the part of 'Ulysses' that Lewis used to recite so divinely. The last line is one of the greatest challenges I know:

To strive, to seek, to find, and not to yield.

I did not discover the poems of Gerard Manley Hopkins until late in life and then I was thrilled by them. 'The Habit of Perfection' is to me a perfect poem. All his verse is touched with humour and the realisation of the presence of God in everything, small or great. His superb characterisation in 'Felix Randal' is hard to beat. I think this poem represents a nurse or someone who has been looking after him, a monk or a nun perhaps.

'Nightingales' and 'A Passer-by' were some of Lewis's special favourites and he spoke them so superbly that I cannot bear to hear anyone else speak them. I read them aloud to myself sometimes — but never in public.

'Oh what know they of harbours' is a personal poem to Lewis and myself. It expresses such affection and longing. He and I would say it to each other often. The last verse conveys the bond of love so movingly.

'As I went down to Dymchurch Wall' has a special place in my affections, because Dymchurch was our country home when I was young, and I discovered that Lewis also knew and loved the place as a boy. Popular at our recitals was 'Roundabouts and Swings' — so simple and funny. It sounds best spoken with a trace of local dialect in the speech. Vivid pictures, characterisation and a lovely lilt make this great fun to do.

Yeats' 'When you are old' is another poem that Lewis and I loved for personal reasons — it is so apt for married couples. Yeats had great poignancy and sadness in his verse: 'I will arise and go now, and go to Innisfree' and 'Down by the salley gardens' are full of homesickness. I heard Yeats speak his own poems but I'm afraid that he didn't do them very well!

After a mild summer like that of 1972 the autumn trees were particularly beautiful and Herbert Trench's poem 'O dreamy, gloomy, friendly trees . . .' sprang to mind on many occasions. In complete contrast I have chosen 'A poor lad once and a lad so trim', his semi-humorous poem with a sting in the last line.

The two poems by James Stephens I include because I do appreciate his tremendous compassion for living creatures and his sense of humour.

With John Masefield we come to a poet that Lewis in particular loved. 'Twilight' I know he had a special affection for, while I like best 'The Everlasting Mercy'. Here I have selected only a part, though I have read the whole work at a recital. These verses are vivid, steeped with meaning. Here is a prayer, moving, cruel and yet so merciful; carved right out of the earth itself by the people who work with the soil.

'A late lark twitters' holds a unique place in our affections. Lewis asked that it be read at his funeral and our son John read it beautifully. I have asked that it be read at mine.

John is the poet in the family. He sent these two poems to us when he was in a prisoner of war camp during the Second World War. In these lines he was remembering with nostalgia the aspects of flying which he loved, the freedom, and the feeling of power. Yet there is anguish too in remembering the havoc that was wreaked by the bombing.

I have linked next the more recent writings of an Irishman, a Welshman and a Scot. In choosing two speeches from Shaw's *St Joan* I am recalling one of the peaks of my career, because this play was written with me in mind. Bernard Shaw refused to write the play until he had seen someone who could play the part of Joan. This was despite the fact that his wife had collected all the material and had been urging him to write it. Then he saw us play the trial scene from Shelley's *Beatrice Cenci* and he went home to Mrs Shaw and said "I've found the girl who can play Joan." Perhaps he didn't say "girl" — I was 42! In 1924 I performed the play knowing that every word was authentic, based on the historical records of the trial, with the exception of these two absolutely original speeches which Shaw created for Joan. To me these are pure poetry — yet the critics said Shaw wasn't a poet!

By contrast I have included a delightfully droll poem from Dylan Thomas's *Under Milk Wood*, remembering how well Lewis did this with a pronounced Welsh accent. I try to do it now but don't succeed nearly so well.

With Hugh MacDiarmid, I feel we have come to the best of modern Scottish poetry that began its proud journey with the old ballads at the beginning. Hugh MacDiarmid writes in the Doric mode, not easy for English readers to follow, but if you have a Northern Scot for a grandfather it is a help. 'I heard Christ sing' has all the things I admire in good poetry — rhythm, lilt, gaiety — and yet spiritual depth. Here is a lovely poem of forgiveness, beautifully expressed when Judas and Christ face each other in the last verse. I have met the poet and treasure the book of his poems he gave me.

'Carcassone' completes my selection because it is the poem for which we had the most requests. Frequently letters arrive asking where a copy of it may be obtained. Sadly it is no longer in print and I am glad therefore to include it here. Wherever we went Lewis was asked to do this. I remember the former Prime Minister of Australia, Robert Menzies, meeting us on tour.

"Is Lewis going to do 'Carcassone'?" he said to me.

"No, not tonight!"

"Then I'm not coming." he replied. So I said that of course we would put it in!

And Lewis recited this so well! The little old peasant is delight-fully naive and Lewis put on an old voice to make him sound about seventy, even though he was ninety at the time. But perhaps the most poignant thing of all is that we both longed to visit Carcassone in Southern France, and never managed to. We saw it only on a picture postcard sent to us by our children. On the back they wrote "We are here in Carcassone for twenty-four hours, and it's superb!" and they added the original words of the old French ballad from which this poem is taken, then all four of them signed it. And Lewis and I — "we had meant to go but yet had never gone."

Looking at my selection of favourites I am struck by the vitality and simplicity of these poems. All of them are rooted in real living life — nature, people, incidents, history, character — yet are invaded and filled with spiritual meaning. There is no trace of fantasy here — only the otherworldliness of God's presence in His world. I hope you enjoy reading them.

Sybil Thorndike Casson.

1. EURIPIDES

translated by Gilbert Murray

From THE HIPPOLYTUS

Could I take me to some cavern for mine hiding,
  In the hill-tops where the Sun scarce hath trod;
Or a cloud make the home of mine abiding,
  As a bird among the bird-droves of God!
    Could I wing me to my rest amid the roar
    Of the deep Adriatic on the shore,
Where the waters of Eridanus are clear,
  And Phaethon's sad sisters by his grave
Weep into the river, and each tear
  Gleams, a drop of amber, in the wave.

To the strand of the Daughters of the Sunset,
  The apple-tree, the singing and the gold;
Where the mariner must stay him from his onset,
  And the red wave is tranquil as of old;
    Yea, beyond that Pillar of the End
    That Atlas guardeth, would I wend;
Where a voice of living waters never ceaseth
  In God's quiet garden by the sea,
And earth, the ancient life-giver, increaseth
  Joy among the meadows, like a tree.

From MEDEA

Medea, having been rejected by the father of her children:

Women, my mind is clear. I go to slay
My children with all speed, and then, away
From hence; not wait yet longer till they stand
Beneath another and an angrier hand
To die. Yea, howso'er I shield them, die
They must. And, seeing that they must, 'tis I
Shall slay them, I their mother, touched of none
Beside. Oh, up, and get thine armour on,
My heart! Why longer tarry we to win
Our crown of dire inevitable sin?
Take up thy sword, O poor right hand of mine,
Thy sword: then onward to the thin-drawn line
Where life turns agony. Let there be naught
Of softness now: and keep thee from that thought,
"Born of thy flesh," "thine own beloved." Now,
For one brief day forget thy children: thou
Shalt weep hereafter. Though thou slay them, yet
Sweet were they . . . I am sore unfortunate.

From THE TROJAN WOMEN

Hecuba:
Lo, I have seen the open hand of God;
And in it nothing, nothing, save the rod
Of mine affliction, and the eternal hate,
Beyond all lands, chosen and lifted great
For Troy! Vain, vain were prayer and incense-swell
And bull's blood on the altars! . . . All is well.
Had he not turned us in His hand, and thrust
Our high things low and shook our hills as dust,
We had not been this splendour, and our wrong
An everlasting music for the song
Of earth and heaven!
                        Go, women; lay our dead
In his low sepulchre. He hath his meed
Of robing. And, methinks, but little care
Toucheth the tomb, if they that moulder there
Have rich encerement. 'Tis we, 'tis we,
That dream, we living and our vanity!

2. ANONYMOUS

Of a rose, a lovely rose, Of a rose is al myn song
Lestenyt, lordynges, both elde and yinge,
How this rose began to sprynge;
Swych a rose to myn lykynge
   In al this world ne knowe I non.

The Aungil came fro hevene tour,
To grete Marye with great honour,
And seyde sche xuld bere the flour
   That xulde breke the fyndes bond.

The flour sprong in heye Bedlem,
That is bothe bryht and schen:
The rose is Mary, hevene qwen,
   Out of here bosum the blosme sprong.

The ferste braunche is ful of myht,
The sprong on Cyrstemesse nyht,
The sterre schon over Bedlem bryht
   That is bothe brod and long.

The secunde braunche sprong to helle,
The fendys power doun to felle:
Therein myht non sowle dwelle;
   Blyssid be the time the rose sprong!

The thredde braunche is good and swote,
It sprang to hevene, crop and rote,
Therein to dwellyn and ben our bote;
   Every day it schewit in prystes hond.

Prey we to here with gret honour,
She that bar the blyssid flowr,
She be our helpe and our socour
   And schyld us fro the fyndes bond.

May in the Green-Wood

In somer when the shawes be sheyne,
　And leves be large and long,
Hit is full merry in feyre foreste
　To here the foulys song.

　To se the dere draw to the dale
And leve the hilles hee,
And shadow him in the leves grene
　Under the green-wode tree.

Hit befell on Whitsontide
　Early in a May mornyng,
The Sonne up faire can shyne,
　And the briddis mery can syng.

'This is a mery mornyng,' said Litulle Johne,
　'Be Hym that dyed on tre;
A more mery man than I am one
　Lyves not in Christiantè.

'Pluk up thi hert, me dere mayster,'
　Litulle Johne can say,
'And thynk hit is a fulle fayre tyme
　In a mornynge of May.'

Carol

I sing of a maiden
   That is makeles;
King of all kings
   To her son she ches.

He came al so still
   There his mother was,
As dew in April
   That falleth on the grass.

He came al so still
   To his mother's bour.
As dew in April
   That falleth on the flour.

He came al so still
   There his mother lay,
As dew in April
   That falleth on the spray.

Mother and maiden
   Was never none but she;
Well may such a lady
   Goddes mother be.

Balow

Balow, my babe, lie still and sleep!
It grieves me sore to see thee weep.
Wouldst thou be quiet I'se be glad,
Thy mourning makes my sorrow sad:
Balow my boy, thy mother's joy,
Thy father breeds me great annoy —
　　　　　　　　Balow, la-low!

When he began to court my love,
And with his sugred words me move,
His fainings false and flattering cheer
To me that time did not appear:
But now I see most cruelly
He cares ne for my babe nor me —
　　　　　　　　Balow, la-low!

Lie still, my darling, sleep awhile,
And when thou wak'st thou'le sweetly smile:
But smile not as thy father did,
To cozen maids: ney, God forbid!
But yet I fear thou wilt go near
Thy father's heart and face to bear—
　　　　　　　　Balow, la-low!

I cannot choose but ever will
Be loving to thy father still;
Where'er he go, where'er he ride,
My love with him doth still abide;
In weal or woe, where'er he go,
My heart shall ne'er depart him fro —
                    Balow, la-low!

But do not, do not, pretty mine,
To faynings false thy heart incline!
Be loyal to thy lover true,
And never change her for a new:
If good or fair, of her have care
For women's banning's wondrous sare —
                    Balow, la-low!

Bairn, by thy face I will beware;
Like Sirens' words, I'll come not near;
My babe and I together will live;
He'll comfort me when cares do grieve.
My babe and I right soft will lie,
And ne'er respect man's crueltye —
                    Balow, la-low!

Farewell, farewell, the falsest youth
That ever kist a woman's mouth!
I would all maids be warn'd by me
Never to trust man's curtesye;
For if we do but chance to bow,
They'll treat us then they care not how —
Balow, la-low!

The Old Cloak

This winter's weather it waxeth cold,
   And frost it freezeth on every hill,
And Boreas blows his blast so bold
   That all our cattle are like to spill.
Bell, my wife, she loves no strife;
   She said unto me quietlye,
Rise up, and save cow Crumbock's life!
   Man, put thine old cloak about thee!

He   O Bell my wife, why dost thou flyte?
   Thou knowst my cloak is very thin:
It is so bare and over worn,
   A cricket thereon cannot renn.
Then I'll no longer borrow nor lend;
   For once I'll new apparell'd be;
To-morrow I'll to town and spend;
   For I'll have a new cloak about me.

She   Cow Crumbock is a very good cow:
   She has been always true to the pail;
She has helped us to butter and cheese, I trow,
   And other things she will not fail.
I would be loth to see her pine.
   Good husband, counsel take of me:
It is not for us to go so fine —
   Man, take thine old cloak about thee!

34

He   My cloak it was a very good cloak,
          It hath been always true to the wear;
      But now it is not worth a groat:
          I have had it four and forty year'.
      Sometime it was of cloth in grain:
          'Tis now but a sigh clout, as you may see:
      It will neither hold out wind nor rain;
          And I'll have a new cloak about me.

She   It is four and forty years ago
          Sine the one of us the other did ken;
      And we have had, betwixt us two,
          Of children either nine or ten:
      We have brought them up to women and men:
          In the fear of God I trow they be.
      And why wilt thou thyself misken?
          Man, take thine old cloak about thee!

He   O Bell my wife, why dost thou flyte?
          Now is now, and then was then:
      Seek now all the world throughout,
          Thou kens not clowns from gentlemen;
      They are clad in black, green, yellow and blue,
          So far above their own degree.
      Once in my life I'll take a view;
          For I'll have a new cloak about me.

She   King Stephen was a worthy peer;
           His breeches cost him but a crown;
      He held them sixpence all too dear,
           Therefore he called the tailor 'lown'.
      He was a knight of great renown,
           And thou is but of low degree:
      It's pride that puts this country down:
           Man, take thy old cloak about thee!

He   Bell my wife, she loves not strife,
           Yet she will lead me, if she can;
      And to maintain an easy life
           I oft must yield, though I'm good-man.
      It's not for a man with a woman to threap,
           Unless he first give o'er the plea;
      As we began, so will we keep,
           And I'll take my old cloak about me.

The Bonnie House o' Airlie

It fell on a day, and a bonnie simmer day,
    When green grew aits and barley,
That there fell out a great dispute
    Between Argyll and Airlie.

Argyll has raised an hunder men,
    An hunder harness'd rarely,
And he's awa' by the back of Dunkell,
    To plunder the castle of Airlie.

Lady Ogilvie looks o'er her bower-window,
    And O but she looks warely!
And there she spied the great Argyll,
    Come to plunder the bonnie house of Airlie.

'Come down, come down, my Lady Ogilvie,
    Come down and kiss me fairly':
'O I winna kiss the fause Argyll,
    If he shouldna leave a standing stane in Airlie.'

He hath taken her by the left shoulder,
    Says, 'Dame, where lies thy dowry?'
'O it's east and west yon wan water side,
    And it's down by the banks of the Airlie.'

They hae sought it up, they hae sought it down,
  They hae sought it maist severely,
Till they fand it in the fair plum-tree
  That shines on the bowling-green of Airlie.

He hath taken her by the middle sae small,
  And O but she grat sairly?
And laid her down by the bonnie burn-side,
  Till they plunder'd the castle of Airlie.

'Gif my gude lord war here this night,
  As he is with King Charlie,
Neither you, nor ony ither Scottish lord,
  Durst avow to the plundering of Airlie.

'Gif my gude lord war now at home,
  As he is with his king,
There durst nae a Campbell in a' Argyll
  Set fit on Airlie green.

'Ten bonnie sons I have borne unto him,
  The eleventh ne'er saw his daddy;
But though I had an hunder mair,
  I'd gie them a' to King Charlie!'

A Lyke-Wake Dirge

This ae nighte, this ae nighte,
  Every nighte and alle,
Fire and fleet and candle-lighte.
  And Christe receive thy saule.

When thou from hence away art past,
  Every nighte and alle,
To Whinny-muir thou com'st at last;
  And Christe receive thy saule.

If ever thou gavest hosen and shoon,
  Every nighte and alle,
Sit thee down and put them on;
  And Christe receive thy saule.

If hosen and shoon thou ne'er gav'st nane
  Every nighte and alle,
The whinnes sall prick thee to the bare bane;
  And Christe receive thy saule.

From Whinny-muir when thou may'st pass,
  Every nighte and alle,
To Brig o' Dread thou com'st at last;
  And Christe receive thy saule.

From Brig o' Dread when thou may'st pass,
Every nighte and alle,
To Purgatory fire thou com'st at last;
And Christe receive thy saule.

If ever thou gavest meat or drink,
Every nighte and alle,
The fire sall never make thee shrink;
And Christe receive thy saule.

If meat or drink thou ne'er gav'st nane,
Every nighte and alle,
The fire will burn thee to the bare bane;
And Christe receive they saule.

This ae nighte, this ae nighte,
Every nighte and alle,
Fire and fleet and candle-lighte,
And Christe receive thy saule.

The Seven Virgins—A Carol

All under the leaves and the leaves of life
    I met with virgins seven,
And one of them was Mary mild,
    Our Lord's mother of Heaven.

'O what are you seeking, you seven fair maids,
    All under the leaves of life?
Come tell, come tell, what seek you
    All under the leaves of life?'

'We're seeking for no leaves, Thomas,
    But for a friend of thine;
We're seeking for sweet Jesus Christ,
    To be our guide and thine.'

'Go down, go down, to yonder town,
    And sit in the gallery,
And there you'll see sweet Jesus Christ,
    Nail'd to a big yew-tree.'

So down they went to yonder town
    As fast as foot could fall,
And many a grievous bitter tear
    From the virgins' eyes did fall.

'O peace, Mother, O peace, Mother,
   Your weeping doth me grieve:
I must suffer this,' He said,
   'For Adam and for Eve.

'O Mother, take you John Evangelist
   All for to be your son,
And he will comfort you sometimes,
   Mother, as I have done.'

'O come, thou John Evangelist,
   Thou'rt welcome unto me;
But more welcome my own dear Son,
   Whom I nursed on my knee.'

Then He laid His head on His right shoulder,
   Seeing death it struck Him nigh —
'The Holy Ghost be with your soul,
   I die, Mother dear, I die.'

O the rose, the gentle rose,
   And the fennel that grows so green!
God give us grace in every place
   To pray for our king and queen.

Furthermore for our enemies all
   Our prayers they should be strong;
Amen, good Lord; your charity
   Is the ending of my song.

Two Rivers

Says Tweed to Till —
'What gars ye rin sae still?'
Says Till to Tweed —
'Though ye rin with speed
And I rin slaw,
For ae man that ye droon
I droon twa.'

Cradle Song

O my deir hert, young Jesus sweit,
Prepare thy creddil in my spreit,
And I sall rock thee in my hert
And never mair from thee depart.

But I sall praise thee evermoir
With sangis sweit unto thy gloir;
The knees of my hert sall I bow,
And sing that richt *Balulalow*!

Barbara Allen's Cruelty

In Scarlet town, where I was born,
　There was a fair maid dwellin',
Made every youth cry 'Well-a-way!'
　Her name was Barbara Allen.

All in the merry month of May,
　When green buds they were swellin',
Young Jemmy Grove on his death-bed lay,
　For love of Barbara Allen.

He sent his man in to her then,
　To the town where she was dwellin',
'O haste and come to my master dear,
　If your name be Barbara Allen.'

So slowly, slowly rase she up,
　And slowly she came nigh him,
And when she drew the curtain by —
　'Young man, I think you're dyin'.'

'O it's I am sick and very very sick,
　And it's all for Barbara Allen.'
'O the better for me ye'se never be,
　Tho' your heart's blood were a-spillin'!

'O dinna ye mind, young man,' says she,
    'When the red wine ye were fillin',
That ye made the healths go round and round,
    And slighted Barbara Allen?'

He turn'd his face unto the wall,
    And death was with him dealin';
'Adieu, adieu, my dear friends all,
    And be kind to Barbara Allen!'

As she was walking o'er the fields,
    She heard the dead-bell knellin';
And every jow the dead-bell gave
    Cried 'Woe to Barbara Allen.'

'O mother, mother, make my bed,
    O make it saft and narrow:
My love has died for me to-day,
    I'll die for him to-morrow.

'Farewell,' she said, 'ye virgins all,
    And shun the fault I fell in:
Henceforth take warning by the fall
    Of cruel Barbara Allen.'

Waly, Waly

O wherefore need I busk my heid,
   Or wherefore need I kame my hair?
For my true Love has me forsook,
   And says he'll never loʻe me mair.
O Waly, waly, up the bank,
   And waly, waly, doun the brae,
And waly, waly, yon burn-side,
   Where I and my Love wont to gae!

O Waly, waly, gin love be bonnie
   A little time while it is new!
But when 'tis auld it waxeth cauld,
   And fades awa' like morning dew.
When cockle shells turn siller bells,
   And mussels graw on every tree,
When frost and snaw doth warm us all,
   Then shall my love prove true to me.

I lean'd my back unto an aik,
   I thocht it was a trustie tree;
But first it bow'd and syne it brak —
   Sae my true love did lichtlie me.
Now Arthur's Seat sall be my bed,
   The sheets sall ne'er be 'filed by me;
Saint Anton's well sall be my drink;
   Since my true Love has forsaken me.

Marti'mas wind, when wilt thou blaw,
　　And shake the green leaves aff the tree?
O gentle Death, when wilt thou come?
　　And take a life that wearies me.
'Tis not the frost, that freezes fell,
　　Nor blawing snaw's inclemencie,
'Tis not sic cauld that makes me cry;
　　But my Love's heart grown cauld to me.

When we cam in by Glasgow toun,
　　We were a comely sicht to see;
My Love was clad in the black velvet,
　　And I mysel in cramasie.
But had I wist, before I kist,
　　That love had been sae ill to win,
I had lock'd my heart in a case o' gowd.
　　And pinn'd it wi' a siller pin.

And O! if my young babe were born,
　　And set upon the nurse's knee;
And I myself were dead and gane,
　　And the green grass growing over me!
O Waly, waly, gin love be bonnie
　　A little time while it is new!
But when 'tis auld it waxeth cauld,
　　And fades awa' like morning dew.

The Queen's Marie

Marie Hamilton's to the kirk gane,
    Wi' ribbons in her hair;
The King thought mair o' Marie Hamilton
    Than ony that were there.

Marie Hamilton's to the kirk gane
    Wi' ribbons on her breast;
The King thought mair o' Marie Hamilton
    Than he listen'd to the priest.

Marie Hamilton's to the kirk gane,
    Wi' gloves upon her hands;
The King thought mair o' Marie Hamilton
    Than the Queen and a' her lands.

She hadna been about the King's court
    A month, but barely one,
Till she was beloved by a' the King's court
    And the King the only man.

She hadna been about the King's court
    A month, but barely three,
Till frae the King's court Marie Hamilton
    Marie Hamilton durstna be.

The King is to the Abbey gane,
　　To pu' the Abbey tree,
To scale the babe frae Marie's heart;
　　But the thing it wadna be.

O she has row'd it in her apron,
　　And set it on the sea —
'Gae sink ye or swim ye, bonny babe,
　　Ye'se get nae mair o' me.'

Word is to the kitchen gane,
　　And word is to the ha',
And word is to the noble room
　　Amang the ladies a',
That Marie Hamilton's brought to bed,
　　And the bonny babe's miss'd and awa'.

Scarcely had she lain down again,
　　And scarcely fa'en alseep,
When up and started our gude Queen
　　Just at her bed-feet;
Saying — 'Marie Hamilton, where's your babe?
　　For I am sure I heard it greet.'

'O no, O no, my noble Queen!
    Think no sic thing to be;
'Twas but a stitch into my side,
    And sair it troubles me!'

'Get up, get up, Marie Hamilton:
    Get up and follow me;
For I am going to Edinburgh town,
    A rich wedding for to see.'

O slowly, slowly rase she up,
    And slowly put she on;
And slowly rade she on the way
    Wi' mony a weary groan.

The Queen was clad in scarlet,
    Her merry maids all in green;
And every town that they came to,
    They took Marie for the Queen.

'Ride hooly, hooly, gentlemen,
    Ride hooly now wi' me!
For never, I am sure, a wearier burd
    Rade in your companie,' —

But little wist Marie Hamilton,
  When she rade on the brown,
That she was gaen to Edinburgh town,
  And a' to be put down.

'Why weep ye so, ye burgess wives,
  Why look ye so on me?
O I am going to Edinburgh town,
  A rich wedding to see.'

When she gaed up the tolbooth stairs,
  The corks frae her heels did flee;
And lang or e'er she cam down again,
  She was condemn'd to die.

When she cam to the Netherbow port,
  She laugh'd loud laughters three;
But when she cam to the gallows foot
  The tears blinded her e'e.

'Yestreen the Queen had four Maries,
  The night she'll hae but three;
There was Marie Seaton, and Marie Beaton,
  And Marie Carmichael, and me.

'O often have I dress'd my Queen
    And put gowd upon her hair;
But now I've gotten for my reward
    The gallows to be my share.

'Often have I dress'd my Queen
    And often made her bed;
But now I've gotten for my reward
    The gallows tree to tread.

'I charge ye all, ye mariners,
    When ye sail owre the faem,
Let neither my father nor mother get wit
    But that I'm coming hame.

'I charge ye all, ye mariners,
    That sail upon the sea,
That neither my father nor mother get wit
    The dog's death I'm to die.

'For if my father and mother got wit,
    And my bold brethren three,
O mickle wad be the gude red blude
    This day wad be spilt for me!

'O little did my mother ken,
   When first she cradled me,
That I should die sae far fra hame
   And hang on a gallows tree.'

3. ROBERT MANNYNG OF BRUNNE

Praise of Women

No thynge ys to man so dere
As wommanys love in gode manere.
A gode womman is mannys blys,
There here love right and steadfast is.
There is no solas under hevene
Of alle that a man may nevene
That shuld a man do so moche glew
As a gode womman that loveth trew.
Ne derer is none in Goddys hurde
Than a chaste womman with lovely worde.

4. *WILLIAM DUNBAR*

From   *Lament for the Makers*

I that in heill was and gladness
And trublit now with great sickness
And feblit with infirmitie:
    Timor Mortis conturbat me.

Our plesance here is all vain glory,
This fals world is but transitory,
The flesh is bruckle, the Feynd is slee:
    Timor Mortis conturbat me.

The state of man does change and vary,
Now sound, now sick, now blyth, now sary,
Now dansand mirry, now like to die:
    Timor Mortis conturbat me.

Unto the Death gois all Estatis,
Princis, Prelatis, and Potestatis,
Baith rich and poor of all degree:
    Timor Mortis conturbat me.

He spairis no lord for his piscence,
Na clerk for his intelligence;
His awful straik may no man flee:
Timor Mortis conturbat me.

L   Art-magicianis and astrologgis,
Rethoris, logicianis, and theologgis,
Them helpis no conclusionis slee:
Timor Mortis conturbat me.

S   In medecine the most practicianis,
Leechis, surrigianis, and physicianis,
Themself from Death may not supplee:
Timor Mortis conturbat me.

L   I see that makaris amang the lave
Playis here their padyanis, syne gois to grave;
Sparit is nocht their facultie:
Timor Mortis conturbat me.

S He has done petuously devour
 The noble Chaucer, of makaris flour,
 The Monk of Bury, and Gower, all three:
  Timor Mortis conturbat me.

L That scorpion fell has done infeck
 Maister John Clerk and James Afflek,
 Fra ballat-making and tragedie:
  Timor Mortis conturbat me.

S He has tane Rowll of Aberdene,
 And gentill Rowll of Corstorphine;
 Two better fallowis did no man see:
  Timor Mortis conturbat me.

L And he has now tane, last of al,
 Good gentil Stobo and Quintin Shaw,
 Of quhom all wichtis hes pitie:
  Timor Mortis conturbat me.

S   Good Maister Walter Kennedy
In point of Death lies verily;
Great ruth it were that so suld be:
   Timor Mortis conturbat me.

L   Sen he has all my brether tane,
He will naught let me live alane;
Of force I man his next prey be:
   Timor Mortis conturbat me.

S   Since for the Death remeid is none,
Best is that we for Death dispone,
After our death that live may we:
   Timor Mortis conturbat me.

5. SIR WALTER RALEIGH

His Pilgrimage

Give me my scallop-shell of quiet,
    My staff of faith to walk upon,
My scrip of joy, immortal diet,
    My bottle of salvation,
My gown of glory, hope's true gage;
And thus I'll take my pilgrimage.

Blood must be my body's balmer;
    No other balm will there be given;
Whilst my soul, like quiet palmer,
    Travelleth towards the land of heaven;
Over the silver mountains,
Where spring the nectar fountains;
        There will I kiss
        The bowl of bliss;
        And drink mine everlasting fill
        Upon every milken hill.
        My soul will be a-dry before;
        But, after, it will thirst no more.

The Conclusion

Even such is Time, that takes in trust
   Our youth, our joys, our all we have,
And pays us but with earth and dust;
   Who in the dark and silent grave,
When we have wander'd all our ways,
Shuts up the story of our days;
But from this earth, this grave, this dust,
My God shall raise me up, I trust.

6. EDMUND SPENSER

A Ditty
In praise of Eliza, Queen of the Shepherds

See where she sits upon the grassie greene,
    (O seemely sight!)
Yclad in Scarlot, like a mayden Queene,
    And ermines white:
Upon her head a Cremosin coronet
With Damaske roses and Daffadillies set:
    Bay leaves betweene
    And primroses greene,
Embellish the sweete Violet.

Tell me, have ye seene her angelick face
    Like Phoebe fayre?
Her heavenly haveour, her princely grace,
    Can you well compare?
The Redde rose medled with the White yfere,
In either cheeke depeincten lively chere:
    Her modest eye,
    Her Majestie,
Where have you seene the like but there?

I see Calliope speede her to the place,
　　Where my Goddesse shines;
And after her the other Muses trace
　　With their Violines.
Bene they not Bay braunches which they do beare,
All for Eliza in her hand to weare?
　　So sweetely they play,
　　And sing all the way,
That it a heaven is to heare.

Lo, how finely the Graces can it foote
　　To the Instrument:
They dauncen deffly, and singen soote,
　　In their meriment.
Wants not a fourth Grace to make the daunce even?
Let that rowme to my Lady be yeven.
　　She shal be a Grace,
　　To fyll the fourth place,
And Reigne with the rest in heaven.

Bring hether the Pincke and purple Cullambine,
        With Gelliflowers;
Bring Coronations, and Sops-in-wine
        Worne of Paramoures:
Strowe me the ground with Daffadowndillies,
And Cowslips, and Kingcups, and lovèd Lillies:
        The pretie Pawnce,
        And the Chevisaunce,
Shall match with the fayre flowre Delice.

Now ryse up, Elisa, deckèd as thou art
        In royall aray;
And now ye daintie Damsells may depart
        Eche one her way.
I feare I have troubled your troupes to longe:
Let dame Elisa thanke you for her song:
        And if you come hether
        When Damsines I gether,
I will part them all you among.

E

7. *WILLIAM SHAKESPEARE*

Silvia

Who is Silvia? What is she?
  That all our swains commend her?
Holy, fair, and wise is she;
  The heavens such grace did lend her,
That she might admirèd be.

Is she kind as she is fair?
  For beauty lives with kindness:
Love doth to her eyes repair,
  To help him of his blindness;
And, being help'd, inhabits there.

Then to Silvia let us sing,
  That Silvia is excelling;
She excels each mortal thing
  Upon the dull earth dwelling:
To her let us garlands bring.

Spring and Winter

i

When daisies pied and violets blue,
  And lady-smocks all silver-white,
And cuckoo-buds of yellow hue
  Do paint the meadows with delight,
The cuckoo then, on every tree,
Mocks married men: for thus sings he,
       Cuckoo!
Cuckoo, cuckoo! — O word of fear,
Unpleasing to a married ear!

When shepherds pipe on oaten straws,
  And merry larks are ploughmen's clocks,
When turtles tread, and rooks, and daws,
  And maidens bleach their summer smocks
The cuckoo then, on every tree,
Mocks married men; for thus sings he,
       Cuckoo!
Cuckoo, cuckoo! — O word of fear,
Unpleasing to a married ear!

Spring and Winter

ii

When icicles hang by the wall,
  And Dick the shepherd blows his nail,
And Tom bears logs into the hall,
  And milk comes frozen in the pail,
When blood is nipp'd, and ways be foul,
Then nightly sings the staring owl,
        To-whit!
To-who! — a merry note,
While greasy Joan doth keel the pot.

When all aloud the wind doth blow,
  And coughing drowns the parson's saw,
And birds sit brooding in the snow,
  And Marian's nose looks red and raw,
When roasted crabs hiss in the bowl,
Then nightly sings the staring owl,
        To whit!
To-who! — a merry note,
While greasy Joan doth keel the pot.

Aubade

Hark! hark! the lark at heaven's gate sings,
    And Phoebus 'gins arise,
His steeds to water at those springs
    On chaliced flowers that lies;
And winking Mary-buds begin
    To ope their golden eyes:
With everything that pretty bin,
    My lady sweet, arise!
      Arise, arise!

Fidele

Fear no more the heat o' the sun,
    Nor the furious winter's rages;
Thou thy worldly task hast done,
    Home art gone, and ta'en thy wages:
Golden lads and girls all must,
As chimney-sweepers, come to dust.

Fear no more the frown o' the great,
    Thou art past the tyrant's stroke;
Care no more to clothe and eat;
    To thee the reed is as the oak:
The sceptre, learning, physic, must
All follow this, and come to dust.

Fear no more the lightning-flash,
    Nor the all-dreaded thunder-stone;
Fear not slander, censure rash;
    Thou hast finish'd joy and moan:
All lovers young, all lovers must
Consign to thee, and come to dust.

No exorciser harm thee!
Nor no witchcraft charm thee!
Ghost unlaid forbear thee!
Nothing ill come near thee!
Quiet consummation have;
And renownèd be thy grave!

Orpheus

Orpheus with his lute made trees
And the mountain tops that freeze
   Bow themselves when he did sing:
To his music plants and flowers
Ever sprung; as sun and showers
   There had made a lasting spring.

Every thing that heard him play,
Even the billows of the sea,
   Hung their heads and then lay by.
In sweet music is such art,
   Killing care and grief of heart
   Fall asleep, or hearing, die.

Sonnet

Shall I compare thee to a Summer's day?
Thou art more lovely and more temperate:
Rough winds do shake the darling buds of May,
And Summer's lease hath all too short a date:
Sometime too hot the eye of heaven shines,
And often is his gold complexion dimm'd;
And every fair from fair sometime declines,
By chance or nature's changing course untrimm'd:
But thy eternal Summer shall not fade
Nor lose possession of that fair thou owest;
Nor shall Death brag thou wanderest in his shade,
When in eternal lines to time thou growest:
    So long as men can breathe, or eyes can see,
    So long lives this, and this gives life to thee.

Sonnet

When, in disgrace with Fortune and men's eyes,
I all alone beweep my outcast state,
And trouble deaf heaven with my bootless cries,
And look upon myself, and curse my fate,
Wishing me like to one more rich in hope,
Featured like him, like him with friends possest,
Desiring this man's art and that man's scope,
With what I most enjoy contented least;
Yet in these thoughts myself almost despising —
Haply I think on thee; and then my state,
Like to the Lark at break of day arising
From sullen earth, sings hymns at Heaven's gate;
    For thy sweet love rememb'red such wealth brings
    That then I scorn to change my state with Kings.

Sonnet

When to the Sessions of sweet silent thought
I summon up remembrance of things past,
I sigh the lack of many a thing I sought,
And with old woes new wail my dear time's waste:
Then can I drown an eye, unused to flow,
For precious friends hid in death's dateless night,
And weep afresh love's long-since-cancell'd woe,
And moan th' expense of many a vanish'd sight:
Then can I grieve at grievances foregone,
And heavily from woe to woe tell o'er
The sad account of fore-bemoanèd moan,
Which I new pay as if not paid before.
   But if the while I think on thee, dear friend,
   All losses are restored and sorrows end.

Sonnet

What is your substance, whereof are you made,
That millions of strange shadows on you tend?
Since every one hath, every one, one shade,
And you, but one, can every shadow lend.
Describe Adonis, and the counterfeit
Is poorly imitated after you;
On Helen's cheek all art of beauty set,
And you in Grecian tires are painted new:
Speak of the spring and foison of the year,
The one doth shadow of your beauty show,
The other as your bounty doth appear;
And you in every blessèd shape we know.
  In all external grace you have some part,
    But you like none, none you, for constant heart.

Sonnet

How like a Winter hath my absence been
From thee, the pleasure of the fleeting year!
What freezings have I felt, what dark days seen,
What old December's bareness everywhere!
And yet this time removed was summer's time;
The teeming Autumn, big with rich increase,
Bearing the wanton burden of the prime
Like widow'd wombs after their Lord's decease:
Yet this abundant issue seem'd to me
But hope of orphans and unfather'd fruit;
For Summer and his pleasures wait on thee,
And, thou away, the very birds are mute:
    Or if they sing, 'tis with so dull a cheer
    That leaves look pale, dreading the Winter's near.

Sonnet

From you have I been absent in the spring,
When proud-pied April, dress'd in all his trim,
Hath put a spirit of youth in everything,
That heavy Saturn laugh'd and leap'd with him.
Yet nor the lays of birds, nor the sweet smell
Of different flowers in odour and in hue,
Could make me any summer's story tell,
Or from their proud lap pluck them where they grew;
Nor did I wonder at the Lily's white,
Nor praise the deep vermilion in the Rose;
They were but sweet, but figures of delight,
Drawn after you, you pattern of all those.
  Yet seem'd it Winter still, and, you away,
  As with your shadow I with these did play.

Sonnet

Let me not to the marriage of true minds
Admit impediments. Love is not love
Which alters when it alteration finds,
Or bends with the remover to remove:
O no! it is an ever-fixèd mark,
That looks on tempests and is never shaken;
It is the star to every wand'ring bark,
Whose worth's unknown, although his height be taken.
Love's not Time's fool, though rosy lips and cheeks
Within his bending sickle's compass come;
Love alters not with his brief hours and weeks,
But bears it out even to the edge of doom:
    If this be error and upon me proved,
    I never writ, nor no man ever loved.

8. BEN JONSON

Simplex Munditiis

Still to be neat, still to be drest,
As you were going to a feast;
Still to be powder'd, still perfumed:
Lady, it is to be presumed,
Though art's hid causes are not found,
All is not sweet, all is not sound.

Give me a look, give me a face
That makes simplicity a grace;
Robes loosely flowing, hair as free:
Such sweet neglect more taketh me
Than all th' adulteries of art;
They strike mine eyes, but not my heart.

Epitaph

On Salathiel Pavy
A child of Queen Elizabeth's Chapel

Weep with me, all you that read
   This little story;
And know, for whom a tear you shed
   Death's self is sorry.
'Twas a child that so did thrive
   In grace and feature,
As Heaven and Nature seem'd to strive
   Which own'd the creature.
Years he number'd scarce thirteen
   When fates turn'd cruel,
Yet three fill'd zodiacs had he been
   The stage's jewel;
And did act (what now we moan)
   Old men so duly,
As sooth the Parcae thought him one,
   He play'd so truly.
So, by error, to his fate
   They all consented;
But, viewing him since, alas, too late!
   They have repented;

And have sought, to give new birth,
   In baths to steep him;
But, being so much too good for earth,
   Heaven vows to keep him.

9. ROBERT HERRICK

To Violets

Welcome, maids of honour!
　　You do bring
　　In the spring,
And wait upon her.

She has virgins many
　　Fresh and fair;
　　Yet you are
More sweet than any.

You're the maiden posies,
　　And so graced
　　To be placed
'Fore damask roses.

Yet, though thus respected,
　　By and by
　　Ye do lie
Poor girls, neglected.

The Funeral Rites of the Rose

The Rose was sick and smiling died;
And, being to be sancitified,
About the bed there sighing stood
The sweet and flowery sisterhood:
Some hung the head, while some did bring,
To wash her, water from the spring;
Some laid her forth, while others wept,
But all a solemn fast there kept:
The holy sisters, some among,
The sacred dirge and trental sung.
But ah! what sweets smelt everywhere,
As Heaven had spent all perfumes there.
At last, when prayers for the dead
And rites were all accomplishèd,
They, weeping, spread a lawny loom,
And closed her up as in a tomb.

(trental — services for the dead, of thirty masses)

Delight in Disorder

A sweet disorder in the dress
Kindles in clothes a wantonness:
A lawn about the shoulders thrown
Into a fine distraction:
An erring lace, which here and there
Enthrals the crimson stomacher:
A cuff neglectful, and thereby
Ribbands to flow confusedly:
A winning wave, deserving note,
In the tempestuous petticoat:
A careless shoe-string, in whose tie
I see a wild civility:
Do more bewitch me than when art
Is too precise in every part.

The Mad Maid's Song

Good-morrow to the day so fair,
  Good-morning sir, to you;
Good-morrow to mine own torn hair
  Bedabbled with the dew.

Good-morning to this primrose too,
  Good-morrow to each maid
That will with flowers the tomb bestrew
  Wherein my love is laid.

Ah! woe is me, woe, woe is me!
  Alack and well-a-day!
For pity, sir, find out that bee
  Which bore my love away.

I'll seek him in your bonnet brave,
  I'll seek him in your eyes;
Nay, now I think they've made his grave
  I' th' bed of strawberries.

I'll seek him there; I know ere this
  The cold, cold earth doth shake him;
But I will go, or send a kiss
  By you, sir, to awake him.

Pray hurt him not; though he be dead,
　　He knows well who do love him,
And who with green turfs rear his head,
　　And who do rudely move him.

He's soft and tender (pray take heed);
　　With bands of cowslips bind him,
And bring him home — but 'tis decreed
　　That I shall never find him!

10. *JOHN MILTON*

From '*Samson Agonistes*'

Oh how comely it is and how reviving
To the Spirits of just men long opprest!
When God into the hands of thir deliverer
Puts invincible might
To quell the mighty of the Earth, th' oppressour,
The brute and boist'rous force of violent men
Hardy and industrious to support
Tyrannic power, but raging to pursue
The righteous and all such as honour Truth;
He all thir Ammunition
And feats of War defeats
With plain Heroic magnitude of mind
And celestial vigour arm'd...

'*Samson Agonistes*' 2

All is best, though we oft doubt,
What th' unsearchable dispose
Of highest wisdom brings about,
And ever best found in the close,
Oft he seems to hide his face,
But unexpectedly returns
And to his faithful Champion hath in place
Bore witness gloriously; whence Gaza mourns
And all that band them to resist
His uncontroulable intent.
His servants he with new acquist
Of true experience from this great event
With peace and consolation hath dismist,
And calm of mind all passion spent.

From *Hymn on the Morning of Christ's Nativity*

It was the Winter wilde,
While the Heav'n-born-childe,
   All meanly wrapt in the rude manger lies;
Nature in aw to him
Had doff't her gawdy trim,
   With her great Master so to sympathise:
It was no season then for her
To wanton with the Sun her lusty Paramour.

Only with speeches fair
She woo's the gentle Air
   To hide her guilty front with innocent Snow,
And on her naked shame,
Pollute with sinfull blame,
   The Saintly Vail of Maiden white to throw,
Confounded, that her Makers eyes
Should look so neer upon her foul deformities.

But he her fears to cease,
Sent down the meek-eyed Peace,
　　She crown'd with Olive green, came softly sliding
Down through the turning sphear
His ready Harbinger,
　　With Turtle wing the amorous clouds dividing,
And waving wide her mirtle wand,
She strikes a universall Peace through Sea and Land.

No War, or Battails sound
Was heard the World around,
　　The idle spear and shield were high up hung;
The hookèd Chariot stood
Unstain'd with hostile blood,
　　The Trumpet spake not to the armèd throng
And Kings sate still with awfull eye,
As if they surely knew their sovran Lord was by.

But peacefull was the night
Wherin the Prince of light
  His raign of peace upon the earth began:
The Windes with wonder whist,
Smoothly the waters kist,
  Whispering new joyes to the milde Ocean,
Who now hath quite forgot to rave,
While Birds of Calm sit brooding on the charmèd wave.

. . . .

But see the Virgin blest,
Hath laid her Babe to rest.
  Time is our tedious Song should here have ending,
Heav'ns youngest teemèd Star,
Hath fixt her polisht Car,
  Her Sleeping Lord with Handmaid Lamp attending:
And all about the Courtly Stable,
Bright-harnest Angels sit in order serviceable.

11. PERCY BYSSHE SHELLEY

Ode to the West Wind

I

O Wild West Wind, thou breath of Autumn's being
  Thou from whose unseen presence the leaves dead
Are driven like ghosts from an enchanter fleeing,

  Yellow, and black, and pale, and hectic red,
Pestilence-stricken multitudes! O thou
  Who chariotest to their dark wintry bed

The wingèd seeds, where they lie cold and low,
  Each like a corpse within its grave, until
Thine azure sister of the Spring shall blow

  Her clarion o'er the dreaming earth, and fill
(Driving sweet buds like flocks to feed in air)
  With living hues and odours plain and hill;

Wild Spirit, which art moving everywhere;
Destroyer and preserver; hear, O hear!

II

Thou on whose stream, 'mid the steep sky's commotion,
   Loose clouds like earth's decaying leaves are shed,
Shook from the tangled boughs of heaven and ocean,

   Angels of rain and lightning! there are spread
On the blue surface of thine airy surge,
   Like the bright hair uplifted from the head

Of some fierce Maenad, even from the dim verge
   Of the horizon to the zenith's height,
The locks of the approaching storm. Thou dirge

   Of the dying year, to which this closing night
Will be the dome of a vast sepulchre,
   Vaulted with all thy congregated might

Of vapours, from whose solid atmosphere
Black rain, and fire, and hail, will burst: O hear!

III

Thou who didst waken from his summer dreams
   The blue Mediterranean, where he lay,
Lull'd by the coil of his crystalline streams,

   Beside a pumice isle in Baiae's bay,
And saw in sleep old palaces and towers
   Quivering within the wave's intenser day,

All overgrown with azure moss, and flowers
   So sweet, the sense faints picturing them! Thou
For whose path the Atlantic's level powers

   Cleave themselves into chasms, while far below
The sea-blooms and the oozy woods which wear
   The sapless foliage of the ocean, know

Thy voice, and suddenly grow gray with fear,
And tremble and despoil themselves: O hear!

IV

If I were a dead leaf thou mightest bear;
　If I were a swift cloud to fly with thee;
A wave to pant beneath thy power, and share

　The impulse of thy strength, only less free
Than thou, O uncontrollable! if even
　I were as in my boyhood, and could be

The comrade of thy wanderings over heaven,
　As then, when to outstrip thy skiey speed
Scarce seem'd a vision — I would ne'er have striven

　As thus with thee in prayer in my sore need.
O! lift me as a wave, a leaf, a cloud!
　I fall upon the thorns of life! I bleed!

A heavy weight of hours has chain'd and bow'd
One too like thee — tameless, and swift, and proud.

V

Make me thy lyre, even as the forest is:
　What if my leaves are falling like its own?
The tumult of thy mighty harmonies

　Will take from both a deep autumnal tone,
Sweet though in sadness. Be thou, Spirit fierce,
　My Spirit! Be thou me, impetuous one!

Drive my dead thoughts over the universe,
　Like wither'd leaves, to quicken a new birth;
And, by the incantation of this verse,

　Scatter, as from an unextinguish'd hearth
Ashes and sparks, my words among mankind!
　Be through my lips to unawaken'd earth

The trumpet of a prophecy! O Wind,
If Winter comes, can Spring be far behind?

To a Skylark

Hail to thee, blithe spirit!
   Bird thou never wert —
That from heaven or near it
   Pourest thy full heart
In profuse strains of unpremeditated art.

   Higher still and higher
     From the earth thou springest,
   Like a cloud of fire;
     The blue deep thou wingest,
And singing still dost soar, and soaring ever singest.

   In the golden light'ning
     Of the sunken sun,
   O'er which clouds are bright'ning,
     Thou dost float and run,
Like an unbodied joy whose race is just begun.

   The pale purple even
     Melts around thy flight;
   Like a star of heaven,
     In the broad daylight
Thou art unseen, but yet I hear thy shrill delight —

Keen as are the arrows
  Of that silver sphere
Whose intense lamp narrows
  In the white dawn clear,
Until we hardly see, we feel that it is there.

All the earth and air
  With thy voice is loud,
As, when night is bare,
  From one lonely cloud
The moon rains out her beams, and heaven is overflow'd.

What thou art we know not;
  What is most like thee?
From rainbow clouds there flow not
  Drops so bright to see,
As from thy presence showers a rain of melody:-

Like a poet hidden
  In the light of thought,
Singing hymns unbidden,
  Till the world is wrought
To sympathy with hopes and fears it heeded not:

Like a high-born maiden
  In a palace tower,
Soothing her love-laden
  Soul in secret hour
With music sweet as love, which overflows her bower:

Like a glow-worm golden
  In a dell of dew,
Scattering unbeholden
  Its aerial hue
Among the flowers and grass which screen it from the view:

Like a rose embower'd
  In its own green leaves,
By warm winds deflower'd,
  Till the scent it gives
Makes faint with too much sweet these heavy-wingèd thieves:

Sound of vernal showers
  On the twinkling grass,
Rain-awaken'd flowers —
  All that ever was
Joyous and clear and fresh — thy music doth surpass.

Teach us, sprite or bird,
   What sweet thoughts are thine:
I have never heard
   Praise of love or wine
That panted forth a flood of rapture so divine.

   Chorus hymeneal,
      Or triumphal chant,
   Match'd with thine would be all
      But an empty vaunt —
A thing wherein we feel there is some hidden want.

   What objects are the fountains
      Of thy happy strain?
   What fields, or waves, or mountains?
      What shapes of sky or plain?
What love of thine own kind? what ignorance of pain?

   With thy clear keen joyance
      Languor cannot be:
   Shadow of annoyance
      Never came near thee:
Thou lovest, but ne'er knew love's sad satiety.

Waking or asleep,
  Thou of death must deem
Things more true and deep
  Than we mortals dream,
Or how could thy notes flow in such a crystal stream?

We look before and after,
  And pine for what is not:
Our sincerest laughter
  With some pain is fraught;
Our sweetest songs are those that tell of saddest thought.

Yet, if we could scorn
  Hate and pride and fear,
If we were things born
  Not to shed a tear,
I know not how thy joy we ever should come near.

Better than all measures
  Of delightful sound,
Better than all treasures
  That in books are found,
Thy skill to poet were, thou scorner of the ground!

Teach me half the gladness
    That thy brain must know;
Such harmonious madness
    From my lips would flow,
The world should listen then, as I am listening now.

12. JOHN KEATS

Ode to a Nightingale

My heart aches, and a drowsy numbness pains
  My sense, as though of hemlock I had drunk,
Or emptied some dull opiate to the drains
  One minute past, and Lethe-wards had sunk:
'Tis not through envy of thy happy lot,
  But being too happy in thy happiness,
    That thou, light-winged Dryad of the trees,
      In some melodious plot
  Of beechen green, and shadows numberless,
    Singest of summer in full-throated ease.

O for a draught of vintage! that hath been
  Cool'd a long age in the deep-delved earth,
Tasting of Flora and the country-green,
  Dance, and Provençal song, and sunburnt mirth!
O for a beaker full of the warm South!
  Full of the true, the blushful Hippocrene,
    With beaded bubbles winking at the brim,
      And purple-stained mouth;
  That I might drink, and leave the world unseen,
    And with thee fade away into the forest dim:

Fade far away, dissolve, and quite forget
  What thou among the leaves hast never known,
The weariness, the fever, and the fret
  Here, where men sit and hear each other grown;
Where palsy shakes a few, sad, last grey hairs,
  Where youth grows pale, and spectre-thin, and dies;
    Where but to think is to be full of sorrow
      And leaden-eyed despairs;
  Where beauty cannot keep her lustrous eyes,
    Or new Love pine at them beyond to-morrow.

Away! Away! for I will fly to thee,
  Not charioted by Bacchus and his pards,
But on the viewless wings of Poesy,
  Though the dull brain perplexes and retards:
Already with thee! tender is the night,
  And haply the Queen-Moon is on her throne,
    Cluster'd around by all her starry Fays
      But here there is no light,
  Save what from heaven is with the breezes blown
    Through verdurous glooms and winding mossy ways.

I cannot see what flowers are at my feet,
   Nor what soft incense hangs upon the boughs,
But, in embalmed darkness, guess each sweet
   Wherewith the seasonable month endows
The grass, the thicket, and the fruit-tree wild;
   White hawthorn, and the pastoral eglantine;
      Fast-fading violets cover'd up in leaves;
        And mid-May's eldest child,
     The coming musk-rose, full of dewy wine,
      The murmurous haunt of flies on summer eves,

Darkling I listen; and for many a time
   I have been half in love with easeful Death,
Call'd him soft names in many mused rhyme,
   To take into the air my quiet breath;
Now more than ever seems it rich to die,
   To cease upon the midnight with no pain,
     While thou art pouring forth thy soul abroad
      In such an ecstasy!
     Still wouldst thou sing, and I have ears in vain —
      To thy high requiem become a sod.

Thou wast not born for death, immortal Bird!
  No hungry generations tread thee down;
The voice I hear this passing night was heard
  In ancient days by emperor and clown:
Perhaps the self-same song that found a path
    Through the sad heart of Ruth, when, sick for home,
      She stood in tears amid the alien corn;
        The same that ofttimes hath
      Charm'd magic casements, opening on the foam
      Of perilous seas, in faery lands forlorn.

Forlorn! the very word is like a bell
  To toll me back from thee to my sole self!
Adieu! the fancy cannot cheat so well
  As she is famed to do, deceiving elf.
Adieu! Adieu! thy plaintive anthem fades
    Past the near meadows, over the still stream,
      Up the hill-side; and now 'tis buried deep
        In the next valley-glades:
      Was it a vision, or a waking dream?
      Fled is that music:- do I wake or sleep?

Ode on a Grecian Urn

Thou still unravish'd bride of quietness,
   Thou foster-child of Silence and slow Time,
Sylvan historian, who canst thus express
   A flowery tale more sweetly than our rhyme:
What leaf-fringed legend haunts about thy shape
   Of deities or mortals, or of both,
      In Tempe or the dales of Arcady?
    What men or gods are these? What maidens loth?
What mad pursuit? What struggle to escape?
    What pipes and timbrels? What wild ecstasy?

Heard melodies are sweet, but those unheard
   Are sweeter; there, ye soft pipes, play on;
Not to the sensual ear, but, more endear'd,
   Pipe to the spirit ditties of no tone;
Fair youth, beneath the trees, thou canst not leave
   Thy song, nor ever can those trees be bare;
      Bold Lover, never, never canst thou kiss,
Though winning near the goal — yet, do not grieve;
    She cannot fade, though thou hast not thy bliss
For ever wilt thou love, and she be fair!

Ah, happy, happy boughs! that cannot shed
    Your leaves, nor ever bid the Spring adieu;
And, happy melodist, unwearied,
    For ever piping songs for ever new;
More happy love! more happy, happy love!
    For ever warm and still to be enjoy'd,
        For ever panting and for ever young;
All breathing human passion far above,
    That leaves a heart high-sorrowful and cloy'd,
        A burning forehead, and a parching tongue.

Who are these coming to the sacrifice?
    To what green altar, O mysterious priest,
Lead'st thou that heifer lowing at the skies,
    And all her silken flanks with garlands drest?
What little town by river or sea-shore,
    Or mountain-built with peaceful citadel,
        Is emptied of its folk, this pious morn?
And, little town, thy streets for evermore
    Will silent be; and not a soul, to tell
        Why thou art desolate, can e'er return.

O Attic shape! fair attitude! with brede
  Of marble men and maidens overwrought,
With forest branches and the trodden weed;
  Thou, silent form! dost tease us out of thought
As doth eternity! Cold pastoral!
  When old age shall this generation waste,
    Thou shalt remain, in midst of other woe
  Than ours, a friend to man, to whom thou say'st,
'Beauty is truth, truth beauty — that is all
    Ye know on earth, and all ye need to know.'

Fragment of an Ode to Maia
(Written on May-Day, 1818)

Mother of Hermes! and still youthful Maia!
    May I sing to thee
As thou wast hymned on the shores of Baiae?
    Or may I woo thee
In earlier Sicilian? or thy smiles
Seek as they once were sought, in Grecian isles,
By bards who died content on pleasant sward,
  Leaving great verse unto a little clan?
O give me their old vigour! and unheard
  Save of the quiet primrose, and the span
    Of heaven, and few ears,
Rounded by thee, my song should die away
    Content as theirs,
Rich in the simple worship of a day.

On first looking into Chapman's Homer

Much have I travell'd in the realms of gold,
  And many goodly states and kingdoms seen;
  Round many western islands have I been
Which bards in fealty to Apollo hold.
Oft of one wide expanse had I been told
  That deep-brow'd Homer ruled as his demesne:
  Yet did I never breathe its pure serene
Till I heard Chapman speak out loud and bold:
Then felt I like some watcher of the skies
  When a new planet swims into his ken;
Or like stout Cortez, when with eagle eyes
  He stared at the Pacific — and all his men
Look'd at each other with a wild surmise —
  Silent, upon a peak in Darien.

13. ROBERT BROWNING

Up at a Villa

I

Had I but plenty of money, money enough and to spare,
The house for me, no doubt, were a house in the city square.
O, such a life, such a life as one leads at the windows there!

II

Something to see, by Baachus, something to hear, at least.
Although there all day long, one's life is a perfect feast.
While up at the villa, one lives, I maintain it, no more than a beast.

III

Well now, look at our villa! Stuck like the horn of a bull
Just on a mountain's edge, bare as a creature's skull,
Save a mere shaggy bush with barely a leaf to pull.
Huh! I scratch my own sometimes to see if the hair has turned
wool.

IV

But the city, oh, the city: the square with the houses! Why?
They're stone-faced, white as a curd — there is something to
catch the eye.
Houses in four straight lines not a single front awry!
You watch who crosses and gossips, who saunters, who hurries by.
Green blinds as a matter of course to draw when the sun gets high.
And the shops with fanciful signs and they're painted properly.

V

And what of the villa? Though winter be over in March by rights.
But it's May ere the snow shall have withered, well off the heights.
You've the brown ploughed land before, where the oxen steam
                      and wheeze,
And the hill over-smoked behind with the pink-grey olive trees.

VI

Is it better in May I ask you? You have summer all at once —
In a day he leaps complete with a few strong April suns.
Mid the short sharp emerald wheat, scarce risen three fingers well,
The wild tulip at end of his tube blows out his great red bell,
Like a thin clear bubble of blood, for the children to pick and sell.

VII

Is it ever hot in the square? There's a fountain to spout and splash,
In the shade it sings and springs. In the shine such foam bows flash
On the horses with curly fish tails, that prance and paddle and plash
Round the lady atop in the conch, that fifty gazers wouldn't abash;
Tho' all she wears is some weeds round her waist in a sort of a
                      sash!

VIII

All the year long at the villa, nothing to see though you linger,
Except yon cypress that points like death's lean lifted forefinger.
Some think fire flies pretty when they mix in the corn and mingle,
Or thread the stinking hemp till the stalks of it seem a-tingle.
Late August, or early September, the stunning cicala is shrill
And the bees keep their tiresome whining round the resinous firs
                                                            on the hill.
Enough of the seasons — I'll spare you the months of the fever
                                                         and chill.

IX

Ere you open your eyes in the city, the blessed church bells begin.
No sooner the bells leave off than the diligence rattles in.
You get the pick of the news and it costs you never a pin!
By the by here's the travelling doctor, gives pills, lets blood,
                                                      draws teeth,
Or the pulcinello trumpet breaks up the market beneath.

At the post office; such a scene picture — a new play, piping hot;
Or a notice how only this morning three liberal thieves were shot;
Above it behold the Archbishop's most fatherly of rebukes;
And beneath, with his crown and his lion, some little new law of
the Dukes.
Or a sonnet, with flowery marge — 'To the Reverend Don.
so-and-so'
Who is Dante Boccaccio Petrarchus St Jerome and Cicero;
And moreover the sonnet goes rhyming — the skirts of St Paul
has reached . . .
Having preached us through six lenten lectures, more unctuous
than ever he preached.
Noon strikes. Here sweeps the procession, Our Lady born smiling
and smart,
With a pink gauze gown, all spangles, and seven swords stuck in
her heart.
Brrm, brrm, brrm, goes the drum, and tootle-te-toot the fife,
There's no keeping one's haunches still; it's the greatest pleasure
in life.

X

But, bless you, it's dear, it's dear; fowls, wine, double the rate;
They've clapped a new tax on salt, and what oil pays passing the
gate:
It's a horror to think of. And so the villa for me not the city;
Beggars can scarcely be choosers, but oh, the pity, the pity!
Look! Two and two go the priests, then the monks with cowls
and sandals,
And the penitents dressed in white shirts holding the yellow
candles.
One, he carries a flag up straight and another, a cross with handles.
And the Duke's guard brings up the rear for the better prevention
of scandals.
Brrm, brrm, brrm, goes the drum and tootle-te-toot the fife,
Oh! a day in the city square — there's no such pleasure in life!

De Gustibus—'

I

Your ghost will walk, you lover of trees,
   (If our loves remain)
   In an English lane,
By a cornfield-side a-flutter with poppies.
Hark, those two in the hazel coppice —
A boy and a girl, if the good fates please,
   Making love, say, —
   The happier they!
Draw yourself up from the light of the moon,
And let them pass, as they will too soon,
   With the bean-flowers' boon,
   And the blackbird's tune,
   And May, and June!

II

What I love best in all the world
Is a castle, precipice-encurled,
In a gash of the wind-grieved Apennine.
Or look for me, old fellow of mine,
(If I get my head from out the mouth
O' the grave, and loose my spirit's bands,
And come again to the land of lands) —
In a sea-side house to the farther South,

Where the baked cicalas die of drouth,
And one sharp tree — 'tis a cypress — stands,
By the many hundred years red-rusted,
Rough iron-spiked, ripe fruit-o'ercrusted,
My sentinel to guard the sands
To the water's edge. For, what expands
Before the house, but the great opaque
Blue breadth of sea without a break?
While, in the house, for ever crumbles
Some fragment of the frescoed walls,
From blisters where a scorpion sprawls.
A girl bare-footed brings, and tumbles
Down on the pavement, green-flesh melons,
And says there's news to-day — the king
Was shot at, touched in the liver-wing,
Goes with his Bourbon arm in a sling:
—She hopes they have not caught the felons.
Italy, my Italy!
Queen Mary's saying serves for me —
　　(When fortune's malice
　　Lost her — Calais) —
Open my heart and you will see
Graved inside of it, 'Italy.'
Such lovers old are I and she:
So it always was, so shall ever be!

A Toccata of Galuppi's

I

Oh Galuppi, Baldassaro, this is very sad to find!
I can hardly misconceive you; it would prove me deaf and blind;
But although I take your meaning, 'tis with such a heavy mind!

II

Here you come with your old music, and here's all the good it
brings.
What, they lived once thus at Venice where the merchants were
the kings,
Where Saint Mark's is, where the Doges used to wed the sea with
rings?

III

Ay, because the sea's the street there; and 'tis arched by . . . what
you call
. . . Shylock's bridge with houses on it, where they kept the
carnival:
I was never out of England — it's as if I saw it all.

IV

Did young people take their pleasure when the sea was warm in
May?
Balls and masks begun at midnight, burning ever to mid-day,
When they made up fresh adventures for the morrow, do you
say?

V

Was a lady such a lady, cheeks so round and lips so red, —
On her neck the small face buoyant, like a bell-flower on its bed
O'er the breast's superb abundance where a man might base his
head?

VI

Well, and it was graceful of them — they'd break talk off and
afford
—She, to bite her mask's black velvet — he, to finger on his
sword,
While you sat and played Toccatas, stately at the clavichord?

VII

What? Those lesser thirds so plaintive, sixths diminished, sigh on
sigh
Told them something? Those suspensions, those solutions —
'Must we die?'
Those commiserating sevenths — 'Life might last! we can but
try!'

VIII

'Were you happy?' — 'Yes.' — 'And are you still as happy?' —
'Yes. And you?'
—'Then, more kisses!' — 'Did I stop them, when a million seemed
so few?'
Hark, the dominant's persistence till it must be answered too!

IX

So, an octave struck the answer. Oh, they praised you, I dare
say!
'Brave Galuppi! that was music! good alike at grave and gay!
I can always leave off talking when I hear a master play!'

X

Then they left you for their pleasure: till in due time, one by one,
Some with lives that came to nothing, some with deeds as well
undone,
Death stepped tacitly and took them where they never see the sun.

XI

But when I sit down to reason, think to take my stand nor swerve,
While I triumph o'er a secret wrung from nature's close reserve,
In you come with your cold music till I creep thro' every nerve.

XII

Yes, you, like a ghostly cricket, creaking where a house was
burned:
'Dust and ashes, dead and done with, Venice spent what Venice
earned.
The soul, doubtless, is immortal — where a soul can be discerned.

XIII

'Yours for instance: you know physics, something of geology,
Mathematics are your pastime; souls shall rise in their degree;
Butterflies may dread extinction ,— you'll not die, it cannot be!

XIV

'As for Venice and her people, merely born to bloom and drop,
Here on earth they bore their fruitage, mirth and folly were the
crop:
What of soul was left, I wonder, when the kissing had to stop?

XV

'Dust and ashes!' So you creak it, and I want the heart to scold.
Dear dead women, with such hair, too — what's become of all
the gold
Used to hang and brush their bosoms? I feel chilly and grown old.

Memorabilia

I

Ah, did you once see Shelley plain,
   And did he stop and speak to you?
And did you speak to him again?
   How strange it seems and new!

II

But you were living before that,
   And also you are living after;
And the memory I started at —
   My starting moves your laughter.

III

I crossed a moor, with a name of its own
   And a use in the world no doubt,
Yet a hand's-breadth of it shines alone
   'Mid the blank miles round about:

IV

For there I picked up on the heather
   And there I put inside my breast
A moulted feather, an eagle-feather!
   Well, I forget the rest.

Home-thoughts, From Abroad

O to be in England
Now that April's there,
And whoever wakes in England
Sees, some morning, unaware,
That the lowest boughs and the brushwood sheaf
Round the elm-tree bole are in tiny leaf,
While the chaffinch sings on the orchard bough
In England — now!

And after April, when May follows,
And the whitethroat builds, and all the swallows!
Hark, where my blossom'd pear-tree in the hedge
Leans to the field and scatters on the clover
Blossoms and dewdrops — at the bent spray's edge —
That's the wise thrush; he sings each song twice over,
Lest you should think he never could recapture
The first fine careless rapture!
And though the fields look rough with hoary dew,
All will be gay when noontide wakes anew
The buttercups, the little children's dower
—Far brighter than this gaudy melon-flower!

14. LORD TENNYSON

From *Ulysses*

There lies the port; the vessel puffs her sail:
There gloom the dark broad seas. My mariners,
Souls that have toil'd and wrought, and thought with me —
That ever with a frolic welcome took
The thunder and the sunshine, and opposed
Free hearts, free foreheads — you and I are old;
Old age hath yet his honour and his toil;
Death closes all: but something ere the end,
Some work of noble note, may yet be done,
Not unbecoming men that strove with Gods,
The lights begin to twinkle from the rocks:
The long day wanes: the slow moon climbs: the deep
Moans round with many voices. Come, my friends,
'Tis not too late to seek a newer world.
Push off, and sitting well in order smite
The sounding furrow; for my purpose holds
To sail beyond the sunset, and the paths
Of all the western stars, until I die.
It may be that the gulfs will wash us down:
It may be we shall touch the Happy Isles,
And see the great Achilles, whom we knew.

Tho' much is taken, much abides; and tho'
We are not now that strength which in old days
Moved earth and heaven; that which we are, we are;
One equal temper of heroic hearts,
Made weak by time and fate, but strong in will
To strive, to seek, to find, and not to yield.

15. *GERARD MANLEY HOPKINS*

God's Grandeur

The world is charged with the grandeur of God.
　It will flame out, like shining from shook foil;
　It gathers to a greatness, like the ooze of oil
Crushed. Why do men then now not reck his rod?
Generations have trod, have trod, have trod;
　And all is seared with trade; bleared, smeared with toil;
　And wears man's smudge and shares man's smell: the soil
Is bare now, nor can foot feel, being shod.

And for all this, nature is never spent;
　There lives the dearest freshness deep down things;
And though the last lights off the black West went
　Oh, morning, at the brown brink eastward, springs —
Because the Holy Ghost over the bent
　World broods with warm breast and with ah! bright wings.

The Habit of Perfection

Elected Silence, sing to me
And beat upon my whorlèd ear,
Pipe me to pastures still and be
The music that I care to hear.

Shape nothing, lips; be lovely-dumb:
It is shut, the curfew sent
From there where all surrenders come
Which only makes you eloquent.

Be shellèd, eyes, with double dark
And find the uncreated light:
This ruck and reel which you remark
Coils, keeps, and teases simple sight.

Palate, the hutch of tasty lust,
Desire not to be rinsed with wine:
The can must be so sweet, the crust
So fresh that come in fasts divine!

Nostrils, your careless breath that spend
Upon the stir and keep of pride,
What relish shall the censers send
Along the sanctuary side!

O feel-of-primrose hands, O feet
That want the yield of plushy sward,
But you shall walk the golden street
And you unhouse and house the Lord.

And, Poverty, be thou the bride
And now the marriage feast begun,
And lily-coloured clothes provide
Your spouse not laboured-at nor spun.

Pied Beauty

Glory be to God for dappled things —
    For skies of couple-colour as a brinded cow;
      For rose-moles all in stipple upon trout that swim;
Fresh-firecoal chestnut-falls; finches' wings;
    Landscape plotted and pieced — fold, fallow, and plough;
      And all trades, their gear and tackle and trim.

All things counter, original, spare, strange;
    Whatever is fickle, freckled (who knows how?)
      With swift, slow; sweet, sour; adazzle, dim;
He fathers-forth whose beauty is past change:
      Praise him.

Felix Randal

Felix Randal the farrier, O he is dead then? my duty all ended,
Who have watched his mould of man, big-boned and hardy-
                                                                handsome
Pining, pining, till time when reason rambled in it and some
Fatal four disorders, flesh'd there, all contended?

Sickness broke him. Impatient he cursed at first, but mended
Being anointed and all; though a heavenlier heart began some
Months earlier, since I had our sweet reprieve and ransom
Tendered to him. Ah well, God rest him all road ever be offended!

This seeing the sick endears them to us, us too it endears.
My tongue had taught thee comfort, touch had quench'd thy
                                                                tears,
Thy tears that touch'd my heart, child, Felix, poor Felix Randal;

How far from then forethought of, all thy more boisterous years,
When thou at the random grim forge, powerful amidst peers,
Didst fettle for the great grey drayhorse his bright and battering
                                                                sandal!

16. ROBERT BRIDGES

Nightingales

Beautiful must be the mountains whence ye come,
And bright in the fruitful valleys the streams, wherefrom
      Ye learn your song:
Where are those starry woods? O might I wander there,
    Among the flowers which in that heavenly air
      Bloom the year long!

Nay, barren are those mountains and spent the streams:
Our song is the voice of desire, that haunts our dreams,
      A throe of the heart,
Whose pining visions dim, forbidden hopes profound,
    No dying cadence nor long sigh can sound,
      For all our art.

Alone, aloud in the raptured ear of men
We pour our dark nocturnal secret; and then,
      As night is withdrawn
From these sweet-springing meads and bursting boughs of May,
    Dream, while the innumerable choir of day
      Welcome the dawn.

A Passer-by

Whither, O splendid ship, thy white sails crowding,
  Leaning across the bosom of the urgent West,
That fearest nor sea rising, nor sky clouding,
  Whither away, fair rover, and what thy quest?
  Ah! soon, when Winter has all our vales opprest,
When skies are cold and misty, and hail is hurling,
  Wilt thou glide on the blue Pacific, or rest
In a summer haven asleep, thy white sails furling.

I there before thee, in the country that well thou knowest,
  Already arrived am inhaling the odorous air:
I watch thee enter unerringly where thou goest,
And anchor queen of the strange shipping there,
  Thy sails for awnings spread, thy masts bare:
Nor is aught from the foaming reef to the snow-capp'd grandest
  Peak, that is over the feathery palms, more fair
Than thou, so upright, so stately and still thou standest.

And yet, O splendid ship, uphail'd and nameless,
   I know not if, aiming a fancy, I rightly divine
That thou hast a purpose joyful, a courage blameless,
   Thy port assured in a happier land than mine.
   But for all I have given thee, beauty enough is thine
As thou, aslant with trim tackle and shrouding,
   From the proud nostril curve of a prow's line
In the offing scatterest foam, thy white sails crowding.

17. ERNEST RADFORD

Plymouth Harbour

Oh, what know they of harbours
   Who toss not on the sea!
They tell of fairer havens,
   But none so fair there be

As Plymouth town outstretching
   Her quiet arms to me;
Her breast's broad welcome spreading
   From Mewstone to Penlee.

Ah, with this home-thought, darling,
   Come crowding thoughts of thee.
Oh, what know they of harbours
   Who toss not on the sea!

18. JOHN DAVIDSON

In Romney Marsh

As I went down to Dymchurch Wall,
 I heard the South sing o'er the land;
I saw the yellow sunlight fall
 On knolls where Norman churches stand.

And ringing shrilly, taut and lithe,
 Within the wind a core of sound,
The wire from Romney town to Hythe
 Alone its airy journey wound.

A veil of purple vapour flowed
 And trailed its fringe along the Straits;
The upper air like sapphire glowed;
 And roses filled Heaven's central gates.

Masts in the offing wagged their tops;
 The swinging waves pealed on the shore;
The saffron beach, all diamond drops
 And beads of surge, prolonged the roar.

As I came up from Dymchurch Wall,
  I saw above the Down's low crest
The crimson brands of sunset fall,
  Flicker and fade from out the west.

Night sank: like flakes of silver fire
  The stars in one great shower came down;
Shrill blew the wind; and shrill the wire
  Rang out from Hythe to Romney town.

The darkly shining salt sea drops
  Streamed as the waves clashed on the shore;
The beach, with all its organ stops
  Pealing again, prolonged the roar.

19. PATRICK R. CHALMERS

Roundabouts and Swings

It was early last September nigh to Framlin'am-on-Sea,
An' 'twas Fair-day come to-morrow, an' the time was after tea,
An' I met a painted caravan adown a dusty lane,
A Pharaoh with his waggons comin' jolt an' creak an' strain;
A cheery cove an' sunburnt, bold o' eye and wrinkled up,
An' beside him on the splashboard sat a brindled terrier pup,
An' a lurcher wise as Solomon an' lean as fiddle-strings
Was joggin' in the dust along 'is roundabouts and swings.

"Goo'-day," said 'e; "Goo'-day," said I; "an 'ow d'you find
                                                things go,
An' what's the chance o' millions when you runs a travellin'
                                                show?"
"I find," said 'e, "things very much as 'ow I've always found,
For mostly they goes up and down or else goes round and round."
Said 'e "The job's the very spit o' what it always were,
It's bread and bacon mostly when the dog don't catch a 'are;
But lookin' at it broad, an' while it ain't no merchant king's,
What's lost upon the roundabouts we pull up on the swings!"

"Goo' luck," said 'e; "Goo' luck," said I; "you've put it past a
doubt;
An' keep that lurcher on the road, the gamekeepers is out;"
'E thumped upon the footboard an' 'e lumbered on again
To meet a gold-dust sunset down the owl-light in the lane;
An' the moon she climbed the 'azels, while a nightjar seemed to
spin
That Pharaoh's wisdom o'er again, 'is sooth of lose-and-win;
For "up an' down an' round," said 'e, "goes all appointed things,
An' losses on the roundabouts means profits on the swings!"

20. *WILLIAM BUTLER YEATS*

When You are Old

When you are old and gray and full of sleep
  And nodding by the fire, take down this book,
  And slowly read, and dream of the soft look
Your eyes had once, and of their shadows deep;

How many loved your moments of glad grace,
  And loved your beauty with love false or true;
  But one man loved the pilgrim soul in you,
And loved the sorrows of your changing face.

And bending down beside the glowing bars,
  Murmur, a little sadly, how love fled
  And paced upon the mountains overhead,
And hid his face amid a crowd of stars.

The Lake Isle of Innisfree

I will arise and go now, and go to Innisfree,
And a small cabin build there, of clay and wattles made;
Nine bean rows will I have there, a hive for the honey bee,
    And live alone in the bee-loud glade.

And I shall have some peace there, for peace comes dropping
                    slow,
Dropping from the veils of the morning to where the cricket
                    sings;
There midnight's all a-glimmer, and noon a purple glow,
    And evening full of the linnet's wings.

I will arise and go now, for always night and day,
I hear lake water lapping with low sounds by the shore;
While I stand on the roadway, or on the pavements gray,
    I hear it in the deep heart's core.

Down by the Salley Gardens

Down by the salley gardens my love and I did meet;
She passed the salley gardens with little snow-white feet.
She bid me take love easy, as the leaves grow on the tree;
But I, being young and foolish, with her would not agree.

In a field by the river my love and I did stand,
And on my leaning shoulder she laid her snow-white hand.
She bid me take life easy, as the grass grows on the weirs;
But I was young and foolish, and now am full of tears.

21. HERBERT TRENCH

O dreamy, gloomy, friendly trees!

O dreamy, gloomy, friendly trees,
   I came along your narrow track
To bring my gifts unto your knees
   And gifts did you give back;
For when I brought this heart that burns —
   These thoughts that bitterly repine —
And laid them here among the ferns
   And the hum of boughs divine,
Ye, vastest breathers of the air,
   Shook down with slow and mighty poise
Your coolness on the human care,
   Your wonder on its toys,
Your greenness on the heart's despair,
   Your darkness on its noise.

Jean Richepin's Song

A poor lad once and a lad so trim,
 Fol de rol de raly O!
  Fol de rol!
A poor lad once and a lad so trim
 Gave his love to her that loved not him.

And says she 'Fetch me tonight, you rogue'
 Fol de rol de raly O!
  Fol de rol!
And says she 'Fetch me tonight you rogue
 Your mother's heart to feed my dog!'

To his mother's house went that young man —
 Fol de rol de raly O!
  Fol de rol!
To his mother's house went that young man
 Killed her, and took the heart, and ran.

And as he was running, look you, he fell
 Fol de rol de raly O!
  Fol de rol!
And as he was running, look you, he fell
 And the heart rolled on to the ground as well.

And the lad, as the heart was a-rolling, heard
    Fol de rol de raly O!
      Fol de rol!
And the lad, as the heart was a-rolling, heard
That the heart was speaking, and this was the word —

The heart was a-weeping and crying so small,
    Fol de rol de raly O!
      Fol de rol!
The heart was a-weeping and crying so small,
'Are ye hurt my child, are ye hurt at all?'

22. *JAMES STEPHENS*

Little things that run and quail

Little things that run and quail
And die in silence and despair,

Little things that fight and fail
And fall in earth, and sea, and air,

All the trapped and frightened little things —
The mouse, the coney, hear our prayer.

As we forgive those done to us,
The lamb, the linnet, and the hare —

Forgive us all our trespasses,
Little creatures everywhere.

The Rivals

I heard a bird at dawn
Singing sweetly on the tree,
That the dew was on the lawn,
And the wind was on the lea;
But I didn't listen to him,
For he didn't sing to me!

I didn't listen to him,
For he didn't sing to me
That the dew was on the lawn,
And the wind was on the lea!
I was singing at the time,
Just as prettily as he!

I was singing all the time,
Just as prettily as he,
About the dew upon the lawn,
And the wind upon the lea!
So I didn't listen to him,
As he sang upon the tree!

23. JOHN MASEFIELD

Twilight

Twilight it is, and the far woods are dim, and the rooks cry and
call,
Down in the valley the lamps, and the mist, and a star over all,
There by the rick, where they thresh, is the drone at an end,
Twilight it is, and I travel the road with my friend.

I think of the friends who are dead, who were dear long ago in
the past,
Beautiful friends who are dead, though I know that death cannot
last;
Friends with the beautiful eyes that the dust has defiled,
Beautiful souls who were gentle when I was a child.

From *The Everlasting Mercy*

I did not think, I did not strive,
The deep peace burnt my me alive;
The bolted door had broken in,
I knew that I had done with sin.
I knew that Christ had given me birth
To brother all the souls on earth,
And every bird and every beast
Should share the crumbs broke at the feast.

O glory of the lighted mind.
How dead I'd been, how dumb, how blind,
The station brook, to my new eyes,
Was babbling out of Paradise,
The waters rushing from the rain
Were singing Christ has risen again.
I thought all earthly creatures knelt
From rapture of the joy I felt.
The narrow station-wall's brick ledge,
The wild hope withering in the hedge,
The lights in huntsman's upper story
Were part of an eternal glory.

O wet red swathe of earth laid bare,
O truth, O strength, O gleaming share,
O patient eyes that watch the goal,
O ploughman of the sinner's soul.
O Jesus drive the coulter deep
To plough my living man from sleep.
Slow up the hill the plough team plod,
Old Callow at the task of God,
Helped by man's wit, helped by the brute
Turning a stubborn clay to fruit,
Hid eyes for ever on some sign
To help him plough a perfect line . . .

I kneeled there in the muddy fallow,
I knew that Christ was there with Callow,
That Christ was standing there with me,
That Christ had taught me what to be,
That I should plough, and as I ploughed
My Saviour Christ would sing aloud,
And as I drove the clods apart
Christ would be ploughing in my heart,
Through rest-harrow and bitter roots,
Through all my bad life's rotten fruits.

O Christ who holds the open gate,
O Christ who drives the furrow straight,
O Christ, the plough, O Christ, the laughter
Of holy white birds flying after,
Lo, all my heart's field red and torn
And Thou wilt bring the young green corn,
The young green corn divinely springing,
The young green corn forever singing;

And when the field is fresh and fair
Thy blessed feet shall glitter there,
And we will walk the weeded field,
And tell the golden harvest's yield,
The corn that makes the holy bread
By which the soul of man is fed,
The holy bread, the food unpriced,
Thy everlasting mercy, Christ.

24. *WILLIAM ERNEST HENLEY*

Margaritae Sorori

A late lark twitters from the quiet skies:
And from the west,
Where the sun, his day's work ended,
Lingers as in content,
There falls on the old, gray city
An influence luminous and serene,
A shining peace.

The smoke ascends
In a rosy-and-golden haze. The spires
Shine and are changed. In the valley
Shadows rise. The lark sings on. The sun,
Closing his benediction,
Sinks, and the darkening air
Thrills with a sense of the triumphing night —
Night with her train of stars
And her great gift of sleep.

So be my passing!
My task accomplish'd and the long day done,
My wages taken, and in my heart
Some late lark singing,
Let me be gather'd to the quiet West,
The sundown splendid and serene,
Death.

25. JOHN CASSON

Ark Royal 1940

The earth is enriched with the early glow
Of a dawn that is fresh and cold,
As wing to wing through the air we go,
With the sky above and the sea below
In a glory of blue and gold.

What more is desired of such a day
Than a power beneath your hand,
To carry you over the clouds and away,
In an exultation that only they
Who fly may understand?

But today the unspeakable wonder brings
No answering cry of joy
To us who carry beneath our wings,
A cargo of most unholy things
That hunger to destroy.

Yonder our goal in the distance lies
Where the sunlight the land is adorning;
And the whole of creation in agony cries
As we thunder our way across the skies
To desecrate the morning.

Night at sea — after flying

Here in the darkness on the bridge tonight
My mind is wandering in thoughts of yesterday:
For then the dazzling universe of light
Was mine, and all alone I found my way
To that great kingdom of the mighty cloud
Where glistening valleys walk with rolling hills,
Greater than greatness, white, eternal, proud.
There heavenly beauty lies and joy that fills
My heart with wild exultant ecstasy.
Would that now I were in humble happiness
Mid ever moving mountains of the sky.
But here I only know a loneliness
And, waiting for the life that dawn may bring,
Exiled, I watch the night, remembering.

26. BERNARD SHAW

SAINT JOAN

Scene V

In the Cathedral of Rheims after the coronation and the successful defeat of the English, Joan is warned that all will disown her unless she recants:

And where would you all be now if I had heeded that sort of truth?

There is no help, no counsel, in any of you.

Yes; I am alone on earth: I have always been alone.

My father told my brothers to drown me if I would not stay to mind his sheep while France was bleeding to death: France might perish if only our lambs were safe.

I thought France would have friends at the court of the King of France; and I find there only wolves fighting for pieces of her poor torn body.

I thought God would have friends everywhere, because He is the friend of everyone; and in my innocence I believed that you who now cast me out would be like strong towers to keep harm from me.

But I am wiser now; and nobody is any the worse for being wiser.

Do not think you can frighten me by telling me that I am alone.

France is alone; God is alone; and what is my loneliness before the loneliness of my country and my God?

I see now that the loneliness of God is His strength: what would He be if He listened to your jealous little counsels?

Well, my loneliness shall be my strength too; it is better to be alone with God: His friendship will not fail me, nor His counsel, nor His love. In His strength I will dare, and dare, and dare, until I die.

I will go out now to the common people, and let the love in their eyes comfort me for the hate in yours.

You will all be glad to see me burnt; but if I go through the fire I shall go through it to their hearts for ever and ever. As so, God be with me!

SAINT JOAN
Scene VI

During the Trial at Rouen, Joan tears up her signed confession after hearing herself condemned to life imprisonment:

Light your fire!
Do you think I dread it as much as the life of a rat in a hole?
My voices were right. Yes: they told me you were fools, and that I was not to listen to your fine words nor trust to your charity.
You promised me my life; but you lied.
You think life is nothing but not being stone dead. It is not the bread and water that I fear; I can live on bread; when have I asked for more? It is no hardship to drink water if the water be clean.
Bread has no sorrow for me, and water no affliction.
But to shut me from the light of the sky and the sight of the fields and flowers; to chain my feet so that I can never again ride with the soldiers nor climb the hills; to make me breathe foul damp darkness and keep from me everything that brings me back to the love of God, when your wickedness and foolishness tempt me to hate Him: all this is worse than the furnace in the Bible that was heated seven times.
I could do without my warhorse; I could drag about in a skirt; I could let the banners and the trumpets and the knights and

soldiers pass me by and leave me behind as they leave the other women, if only I could still hear the wind in the trees, the larks in the sunshine, the young lambs crying through the healthy frost, and the blessed, blessed church bells that bring my angel voices floating to me on the wind. But without these things I cannot live; and by your wanting to take them away from me, or from any human creature, I know your counsel is of the devil, and that mine is of God.

27. DYLAN THOMAS

Rev. Eli Jenkins' Prayer

Every morning when I wake,
Dear Lord, a little prayer I make,
O please to keep Thy lovely eye
On all poor creatures born to die.

And every evening at sun-down
I ask a blessing on the town,
For whether we last the night or no
I'm sure is always touch-and-go.

We are not wholly bad or good
Who live our lives under Milk Wood,
And Thou, I know, wilt be the first
To see our best side, not our worst.

O let us see another day!
Bless us this night, I pray,
And to the sun we all will bow
And say, good-bye — but just for now!

28. HUGH MACDIARMID

I Heard Christ Sing

I heard Christ sing quhile roond him danced
The twal' disciples in a ring,
And here's the dance I saw them dance,
And the sang I heard him sing.

Ane, twa, three, and their right feet heich,
Fower, five, six, and doon wi' them,
Seevin, aucht, nine, and up wi' the left,
Ten, eleevin, twal', and doon they came.

And Christ he stude i' the middle there,
And was the thirteenth man,
And sang the bonniest sang that e'er
Was sung sin' Time began.

And Christ he was the centrepiece,
Wi' three on ilka side.
My hert stude still, and the sun stude still,
But still the dancers plied

O I wot it was a maypole,
As a man micht seek to see,
Wi' the twal' disciples dancin' roon',
While Christ sang like a lintie.

The twal' points o' the compass
Made jubilee roon' and roon',
And but for the click-click-clack o' the feet,
Christ's sang was the only soon'.

And there was nae time that could be tauld
Frae a clock wha's haun's stude still,
Quhile the figures a' gaed bizzin roon'
— I wot it was God's will . . .

O I wot they'll lead the warl' a dance,
And I wot the sang sall be,
As a white sword loupin' at the hert
O' a' eternity.

Judas and Christ stude face to face,
And mair I couldna' see,
But I wot he did God's will wha made
Siccar o' Calvary.

ANONYMOUS

Carcassone

Adapted by Clifford Harrison from an old French song
by Gustave Nadaud

The sun-warmed valley of the Aude leads down
To Carcassone, an ancient Roman town.
Far off above the nearer hills, one sees
The ridges of the Eastern Pyrenees.
Some half way up the valley stands Limoux.
The only thing that once would hurry through
The village, was the stream that gave its name
Unto the vale. The summers went and came;
The seasons changed: but other change was none.
Till ten years had gone. The busy world
Stopped short at Carcassone.

And in this quiet nook in Southern France,
With days that knew small touch of variance,
A peasant lived, who never once had been
More than a few short miles away, nor seen
A larger place than this Limoux. To him
The outside world was mythical and dim.
Toulouse — and Paris — Bordeaux — and Rome —
O yes, they all were there: but this was home.
One place he'd longed to see and only one:-
He'd meant to go, and yet had never gone:
It was the city yonder — Carcassone.

He said, "I'm growing old. Nigh seventy year,
I've lived my life, and worked the months round, here.
And yet — I doubt not wisely — God has willed
My fondest wish should never be fulfilled;
A wish that I have fostered since a lad,
The one desire that I have always had.
But now I know — we learn it often thus
In disappointments that are sore to us —
There's perfect happiness on earth for none.
I shall not have my wish fulfilled for one.
No, I shall never go to Carcassone.

"One sees the town upon a clear, fine day
Beyond the mountains yonder far away.
To reach it you must go across the plain;
Tis five leagues there, and five leagues back again.
They say the road's a good one and I've known
Folks who've gone there all the way alone.
Ah — if the vintage were but good this year! —
The grapes will not turn yellow yet I fear —
But if the sun had only brightly shone
Prosperous the year had been for everyone;
And so I might have gone to Carcassone.

"They tell me that each day, week in, week out,
A week of Sundays, every day, no doubt,
One sees crowds always going up and down,
Hither and thither, all about the town.
And on the promenade and terraces,
Smart dresses, music, everything you please!
Nay — you may even see at one time there
A bishop and two generals! you stare! —
Tis true. A castle, too — a mighty one!
Huge as the palaces of Babylon!
Think of it, sir! — and all in Carcassone!

"The curate he was right, I must confess:
He spoke the very truth, and nothing less —
'We look too high — we want too much' said he —
A sermon to remember — 'for, you see
How often thus by our desires we fall:
Ambition, oh my friends, destroys us all.'
Quite true, But yet I'm sure it must have fall'n to you
To see some men get what they want. Yet be
No whit the worse. Well now that puzzles me.
My god-child — she is married now — has seen
Perpignan — yes sir: and my wife has been
With our son, Francois — not to go alone —
As far (you'll not believe it!) as Narbonne!
And I? — I've never been to Carcassone.

"Is it a foolish and a sinful thing
This wish? Peace and contentment age doth bring
In much — I have my work, when I am strong;
I get to church; and, when the days are long,
I do my bit of gardening. 'Twould be wrong
To say that there is much I regret.
No: still I'm bound to say there lingers yet
That one wish of my boyhood —
Yes, I should like before my life is done —
I should! — I should! — to go to Carcassone!"

"Cheer up, old friend, for go you shall!" I cried.
"Ay, and we'll go together, side by side;
We'll go tomorrow, if the day is fine."
And in a brimming glass of good white wine
We pledge good luck to the auspicious day.
We started. All the world was bright and gay.
The village all came forth to see us start.
We sat beneath the awning in the cart,
And as we passed along a sweet smile shone
Upon his face, as he, to everyone
He met, cried out "I go to Carcassone!"

Down through the valley, and across the plain;
Over the Aude, made hoarse with autumn rain;
Past dusty thickets, where the crickets sing;
And vintage walls were fruit is ripening;
Through busy little towns and villages,
Where folks were sitting underneath the trees;
We drove. The diligence went past anon,
A cart with oxen yoked came slowly on.
And then, just where the crossroads meet in one,
We saw the signpost. Half the way was done.
I pointed out the words "To Carcassone."

But ah! may heaven forgive us all, say I,
For, as we halted in some shade near by,
I turned, I say, to point the signpost out.
He had been silent for some time. A doubt
Struck on me. "Are you tired, old friend?" I said.
He answered not. I touched him — he was dead.
Bells on the harness jingled. Far away,
The great plains sleeping in the sunshine lay.
The road, a long white line, before us shone.
A clock stuck noontide. Half the way was done.
But he — he never went to Carcassone.

Limoux is changed. Since then its quiet ways
Have heard the roar and scream that nowadays
Alters for good or ill all places such
As this. And Carcassone — changed too? — In much
No doubt! but not that Carcassone he sought.
Changing for all, it still is changed in nought:
For it is built upon enchanted ground.
Ah! Who has seen it? Was it ever found?
Think not this peasant only, he alone,
Dreamt of this place: 'tis nigh to everyone.
For all the world there is a Carcassone.